TREASURE IN EARTHEN VESSELS

Walking in the power of your identity in Christ Jesus

Evangelist Francis Boafo

WESTBOW®
PRESS

A DIVISION OF THOMAS NELSON
& ZONDERVAN

Cover image by Sheryl Moran

Unless otherwise indicated, all Scriptures taken from the New King James Version of the Bible.
Scripture marked NIV taken from the HOLY BIBLE, NEW INTERNATIONAL VERSION®. NIV®. Copyright © 1973, 1978, 1984 by International Bible Society. Used by permission of Zondervan. All rights reserved.

WestBow Press books may be ordered through booksellers or by contacting:

WestBow Press
A Division of Thomas Nelson & Zondervan
1663 Liberty Drive
Bloomington, IN 47403
www.westbowpress.com
1 (866) 928-1240

ISBN: 978-1-4908-4299-8 (sc)
ISBN: 978-1-4908-4300-1 (hc)
ISBN: 978-1-4908-4301-8 (e)

Library of Congress Control Number: 2014911828

Printed in the United States of America.

WestBow Press rev. date: 7/3/2014

Contents

Acknowledgments

I give glory to the Lord who provided me the grace to receive from His Spirit what you are about to read in this book. He enabled the eyes of my heart and the spirit of my mind to receive spontaneous thoughts, and to understand what the Lord is saying to His people in this day and time, which we live. His name alone deserves praise forever. Amen!

I give thanks to God for Pastor Mark Estes, who reviewed this book for scriptural integrity.

Introduction

The life of Jesus on the earth established a new order in the worship and service to God. He demonstrated the power of the Kingdom of Heaven as a lifestyle because God's presence was with Him. With your born-again status, God has redeemed and recreated you by the Spirit of adoption to become a part of His light. He has adopted you, born of His Spirit. He calls you by name and given you an identity in Christ Jesus. Therefore, God expects you to orient your life to the demands your new identity places on you. Though you are an earthen vessel, God wants the power of His kingdom to flow through you in your daily life experiences.

Jesus bore the identity of God and you bear Jesus' identity. He baptizes you with the Holy Spirit and with fire. Your new status in Christ introduces you to the realm of the supernatural, the power of the Kingdom of Heaven.

God expects you to embrace the reality of your identity in Christ. He wants you to acknowledge you are part of the chosen generation and of a royal priesthood. You have become a part of a nation of peculiar, holy people and God's own possession. Embed yourself in Jesus so His power can flow through you for the good of people.

It is very important to know who you have become in the One who shed His blood on your behalf. Let your love for Him motivate you to walk in the power that accompanies your identity in Him. Understand the cost of your new identity in Christ Jesus. His shed blood broke the chains of Satan off you, and God brought you into newness of life. Jesus has washed you from all sins and declared you as acquitted from all guilt before the Holy God.

God wants you to cooperate with Him to make you into a ruler and full of Him in this age and in the age to come. Based on who you are in Christ, and where God is taking you, it is unacceptable to slump into a mundane Christian lifestyle, where you fail to yield to the demands and disciplines of who you have become in Christ. There is supernatural power shut up in your new self—your identity in Christ—which must produce a dynamic life in and through you.

Elymas, a magician in Paphos, opposed Paul and Barnabas when Sergius Paulus, a proconsul sought to hear the Gospel. Apostle Paul, filled with the

Holy Spirit, rebuked him and immediately, mist and darkness fell on him and he became blind. Seeing what happened, the proconsul believed (Acts 13:7-12).

Apostle Peter said to a lame man who begged for money at the gate leading to the temple, "Look at us! I have no silver and gold, but what I do have I give to you. In the name of Jesus Christ of Nazareth, rise up and walk!" And he did (Acts 3:1-9). Apostle Peter gave to the lame man the creative power of the Kingdom to which he now belongs, the power of his new identity in Jesus Christ.

As the moon reflects the sun, you reflect Jesus Christ as light in this world, to illuminate the darkness of many people. Your new identity in Christ is in the likeness of God and therefore you are a member of His family of spiritual power agents. The token of God's nature you have received testifies to your eminent exaltation to the place of reigning with Christ. Therefore, learn to handle the promise of your inheritance of God's kingdom with diligence of faith. Heed God's command to live your identity in Christ.

Be excited about your now and future status. God's immeasurable power abides in you! Yield to the demands it places on your life and become a reflection of God's Light, to illuminate the darkness of many in this corrupt world.—**Evangelist Francis Boafo**

Chapter 1
Overview of Your Identity

You are a chosen generation, a royal priesthood, a holy nation, a people for possession, so that you might speak of the praises of Him who has called you out of darkness into His marvelous light. Once you were not a people, but now you are God's people; once you had not received mercy, but now you have received mercy" (1 Peter 2:9-10).

How do people around you know or identify you? Your identity is how others 'relate' to you. Do your parents, children, siblings, or friends know and see you as reflecting the light of your new identity in Christ. Do they see you as loving and humble? Do they identify you as a person of integrity along with other qualities that you can attribute to the light of your new life in Jesus? Do people call you a "Jesus freak" because you exhibit the light you received from Jesus, which is unusual to the day and age of the world?

You have become a co-worker with God to represent His provision for the needs of others in their life issues. God wants your light to lighten the difficulties (darkness) of people in their life issues because you have the light of Christ. Many issues of life, unfortunately, hinder many from realizing God's expectations for their lives.

Therefore, by acknowledgement of your new identity in Christ, your 'belief system' correctly oriented in Him and your new identity reflecting with appropriate humility toward God and others, you will begin to walk in the power of God. The foundation is the power of your new identity in Christ. The whole creation, including the spiritual realm, is waiting in anticipation for you to take your rightful place, to manifest the power of your identity in Christ as a son and a conqueror.

Because you submit to the power of truth, sincerity, love, righteousness, and holiness, you become a vessel God will use to help other people realize their greatness, and even they break off from strongholds. Know that though you are an earthen vessel, God has invested in you an immeasurable great power, the power that resurrected Jesus from the dead. He has done this to show the whole universe the extraordinary power comes from Him and not you.

Acknowledging Where You Are

Your greatness in Christ places a demand on you. Learn to identify and deny any corruption that may exist in some areas of your life due to worldly lusts. The ever-present enmity between your flesh and God's Spirit introduce corruption in your life if permitted. An inner willingness of ignorance (—not growing roots into Christ), self-deceit, subtle cares of life that 'chokes' the seed of God's word becomes the enemy of the light in you.

The Gospel of your salvation did not come only in words, but also in power and the Holy Spirit will help you live in strong conviction of faith (1 Thessalonians 1:5). Let the power and the freedom in Christ's Gospel help you discover the quality of life that the greatness of your identity demands of you.

There is power in Christ's Gospel, available to help you tear down any limiting stronghold in your life. Christ has promised you power to rule over nations. He has promised to make you a pillar in the temple of His God, and a place with Him on His throne (Revelation 3:12, 21).

Your identity in Christ makes you His light and a ruler in training. You are therefore required to acknowledge your privileged position in Christ daily. With His grace, God wants you to overcome anything that could diminish your light and your strength as you contend against your flesh, the world, and even the spiritual adversaries in the unseen world. These adversaries continually try to manipulate your mind with deceptive inspirations. All they seek is to cause you to live far below the significance of your identity in Christ Jesus. They want you to fall from your position as God's representative in training, to mature your identity in Christ.

The works of the flesh opens up doors into your life, and give advantage to the unseen enemies to reintroduce darkness in certain areas of your life again. However, because you are diligent in the pursuit of your identity, the Holy Spirit says you will be full! He will make you rich and will help you reign as a king in this world of darkness (1 Corinthians 4:8).

Therefore, you have to believe what the Bible says about you. You are more than a conqueror through Jesus. In Him, the Father has blessed you with the opportunity to walk in every spiritual blessing in the heavenly places. He has granted to you everything you need for life, including your Christian walk. Yes, these are the facts about who you are in Jesus Christ! God has predestined you to be conformed to the image of this Champion of champions, Conqueror of conquerors, Lord of Lords, King of kings—Jesus Christ!

By virtue of whom God has made you in Christ, you do not have to allow hate, anger, offense, jealousy, pride, or unforgiving to rule in your heart. Otherwise, you become like one who plays with the "chickens" when God wants you to soar with the "eagles", the great men, and women of God. God did not recreate you to play with the chickens! Your status in Christ is grand. You are a ruler in the making and there is nothing common about your current and future status in Christ Jesus. Jesus wants you to walk in the abundant life and to not allow the enemy to steal anything God wants you to have. However, the choice is yours!

Your future looks bright and very enviable in the eyes of the powers that lost their position with God. No wonder you have all the battles, temptations, and daily difficulties. You fight daily to maintain and grow your life of faith and righteousness. These powers of darkness think they can oppose you long enough so you would doubt your worth and identity in Christ. They think they can convince you to desire "bread and butter of Egypt", that is, the ways of the world where you once lived as a slave.

Therefore, contend against their lies meant to make you live unfaithful to God. Subscribing to worldly lifestyles will prove that you lack knowledge of your identity in Christ. Live a faithful life to God! Be strong in your faith in Him and feed on His Word frequently. Stand firm in your challenges because sometimes, in your challenges, God could be leading you to greater glory. Do you remember the life of Joseph during his captivity in ancient Egypt? Though he went through difficult trials, he was ultimately able to declare,

"…but God meant it unto good, to bring to pass, as it is this day, to save much people alive." In your difficult seasons, convince yourself God is able to turn all that the powers of darkness do against you for your good. Moreover, through many tribulations, believers must enter the Kingdom of God (Acts 14:22).

Be strong and courageous! Stand firm because your redeemer has all power and He is with you. His power is greater and mightier than any force in the whole universe, except the One who gave it—His Father. He said His Father is greater than He is (John 14:28). If God be for you, who can be against you, and Christ in you is greater than he who is in the world.

Conflicts in Life—Lessons from David's Life

God anointed David to become the next king of Israel because the then ruling king, Saul, continued to disappoint God. Though this was true, King Saul was still on the throne. Not only that, but the old (Saul) sought to kill the new (David).

God, through Jesus Christ, has delivered you from the dominion of darkness and transferred you into the Kingdom of light. God has anointed you to be conformed into a priest and a king, even a ruler. Though this is true, the kingdom of darkness still lingers on and daily tries to take any advantage that you may give to it to corrupt and kill God's light in you. Jesus said the devil comes to steal, kill, and destroy (John 10:10). He does this to whomever he can. So do not become a victim. Any corruption in your life makes you fleshly/carnal and it leads to death all over again (Romans 8:13). The fleshly mind is hostile to God, for it does not submit to God's law; indeed, it cannot.

Just as the King, Saul sought to kill David, the newly anointed, so the world seeks to diminish the light of life of God in the believer, if it can. The phenomenon here is a mystery. God used the old and passing king to test the newly anointed David. David came upon King Saul and his company who were all caught in a deep sleep. David could have eliminated King Saul and all his company because he was the only object that stood between him and the throne of Israel, and now vulnerable. In addition, David had the advantage, having with him enough disgruntled warriors who were ready, and willing to eliminate King Saul. David refused to eliminate King Saul.

LESSON: *It's possible that you could let Heaven define you as wicked even if you know the truth, but allow the world to define your choices and decisions, and to influence how you live.*

LESSON: *If you have the habit of taking advantage of the vulnerable in life, Heaven sees you as a wicked person.*

If David had eliminated King Saul, he and Saul would have been alike in the eyes of Heaven. David had a life-transforming knowledge of God's purpose for his life and he knew John 3:27 before its time. John the Baptist said in this passage, "A man can receive nothing, unless it has been given him from Heaven." It is therefore very important that you do not do wrong to possess what you think God has ordained for your life. Moreover, a man cannot do wrong to correct what others have done wrong against him. That is a worldly approach to life! You are better than the competitiveness for position and other advantages in the world. Soar with the "eagles".

LESSON: *A revealed knowledge of God helps you discover your significance… your identity in Christ Jesus.*

Chapter 2
A Look at the Origin of Your Identity

As I indicated in chapter one, identity is a set of behavioral characteristics that sets you apart and by which people relate to you. Such behavior defines your individuality or personality. When people identify with another, they identify with the things that they believe in and sometimes they learn and practice some of their ideals or ideologies. Your status as a Christian identifies you with Christ and you have to learn to admire and practice His ideals and ideologies (His Word). God says you are a new man, a new self, and have a new identity, which He imputed to you by virtue of your new birth in Christ Jesus.

What an honor and glory to know you have an identity with the One by whom God created the whole universe. Greater it is to learn and practice His ideals, spelled out in the Word of God, the Bible. In addition, you honor God when you diligently use all His spiritual and material resources to live and walk as He has made you in Jesus Christ. Apostle John said this, "He who says he abides in Him ought himself also so to walk just as He walked" (1John 2:6). How is that possible? It is because of what I will consider in the next few paragraphs, which is how you came to possess your new identity in Christ. God has given you this identity to help you do what He has redesigned for your life in Christ Jesus.

Lessons from Identity in Nature

Growing up as a young boy, I became very interested in nature. I would navigate through the open land of trees where many kinds of birds came to rest. I watched nature always with a very curious and questioning mind. During these times, I gained some insights from nature. Because of my special love for trees, birds, and plants, I discovered that the fruits on any tree differ in size. I also realized that, so long as the fruit on the tree remained undisturbed by strong winds, man, or by fruit-eating birds and insects, it would remain on the tree to reach maturity.

LESSON: *You are one of the branches attached to the True Vine, Jesus Christ. Like the fruit on a vine, what size of do you want to become? The size you become can determine the fruits you can produce. The choice is yours!*

LESSON: *Your willingness to stay in or live through Jesus will protect you to your maturity in Him. In the journey to your maturity, you will know by illumination the glorious dimensions of your identity in Christ. You will develop a desire for more of Him, whose attributes are now your new identity.*

Because you make up your mind to endure and resist every attempt of the "waves" of evils in the world to pluck you off from Christ, you will abide in Him to reach maturity. As you mature, you come to a deeper and a greater understanding of your identity, and your purpose in life as a Christian.

When the fruit on the tree matures, it ripens and eventually falls from the tree. The fruit makes contact with the soil in the ground where it falls. There, detached from the vine, it rots after some time. The seed or seeds inside of the fruit contact the soil and very soon, a young plant emerges that has the same characteristic as the parent tree, except size. The young plant bears the same identity as the parent and has its DNA.

LESSON: *When you mature in Jesus Christ, His attributes become evident in your daily life and lifestyle. Though you are in contact the world, you die to the world and to the flesh. You become a mature son (tree of righteousness), who can stand on your feet and function as the parent (source) of your identity, Jesus Christ.*

God's Likeness (DNA) in Earthen Vessel

In the book of Genesis, God made trees from the soil. Consequently, trees need soil to survive to produce at their full potential. God also created the fish out of water, and they survive only in water (Genesis 1:21). When it came to the creation of man, as the Bible tells us in Genesis 1:26-27 (KJV),

"And God said, Let us make man in our image, after our likeness: and let them have dominion over the fish of the sea, and over the fowl of the air, and over the cattle, and over all the earth, and over every creeping thing that creepeth upon the earth. So God created man in His own image, in the image of God created he him; male and female created he them."

Transfer of DNA

In Genesis 2:7, God formed man from the dust of the ground. Then, God breathed into his nostrils the breath of life. With the breath of God, something that had never existed came into being—the man. The man became a walking, talking, and reasoning being unlike anything God had made on the earth.

The psalmist said, "I will praise You; for I am fearfully and wonderfully made; Your works are marvelous and my soul knows it very well" (Psalm 139:14). The breath of life from God transformed the man that He had made into a new living creature of His kind on the earth; therefore, like the fish to water, the only place, man has true significance and purpose in life is in God Himself.

Man is a branch attached to Jesus, without whom no man can do anything to God's pleasure, "For apart from me you can do nothing" (John 15:5b). It is in God you have true divine fulfillment. You find your completeness and purpose in God through Jesus Christ who has become your life. Outside of Christ, you lose your divine definition or identity. In God alone is true living, which defines how we move and have our being in this life (Acts 17:28).

Because God created man in His image, in His likeness, and by His divine breath, there was an impartation of God's DNA to man. As I indicated in my insights from nature, the young tree has identical characteristics of the parent tree except in size. If the young tree is transplanted to another location, that will not change its ability to grow and produce the same fruit as the parent tree. Therefore, the young plant bears the same identity, or DNA, as the parent tree.

LESSON: *Since, in Christ, God has restored His DNA to you, He expects you to produce His character as fruit of your new life wherever He places you. Your new life in Him is independent of any particular church you attend. Therefore, it is unacceptable to produce worldly fruits just because you may be away from your local church.*

God is immense in His nature; therefore, unlike the parent tree (which is limited), God is limitless. He does not limit the degree His nature can indwell you. Your lifestyle, mindset, and your diligence in the pursuit of Him can indicate how much of Him will indwell you. Jesus is totally submitted to God His Father, hence God's presence indwelled Him without measure. For in Him dwells all the fullness of the Godhead bodily (Colossians 2:9). Consequently, Jesus functioned in the earth as God. In like manner, it is God's desire to fill you with His fullness if out of your yielded life, you make love your lifestyle and you obey His word (Ephesians 3:17-19).

The Corrupted DNA

The impartation of God's DNA to man and man taking on His nature in the earth was significant. Unfortunately, Satan deceived Eve to disobey God in the Garden of Eden. Satan said to Eve in Genesis 3:4-5, "You shall not surely die, for God knows that when you eat of it your eyes shall be opened, and you shall be like God, knowing good and evil."

What an insult! Adam and Eve were already in the likeness of God. However, because they had no knowledge of who they were, Satan played on their ignorance to deceive them. They disobeyed God and sin entered man, leading to the loss of man's spiritual significance.

LESSON: *It is your responsibility to know and understand your identity in Christ. Failure to do so could make you vulnerable to certain diminishing lifestyle, mindsets and life issue in this world.*

For the sin of disobedience, man lost his spiritual significance. The Bible says in Romans 3:23, "For all have sinned and fall short of the glory of God". Loss of glory indicates the loss of man's spiritual significance in relation to God's nature. Another life from Satan corrupted the life of God in man, which brought him far below God's glory. Satan intruded into man's realm with his deceptive tricks causing man to sin against God. Jesus said to the contentious and unbelieving Jews, "You are of your father the devil, and your will is to do your father's desires. He was a murderer from the beginning, and has nothing to do with the truth, because there is no truth in him. When he lies, he speaks out of his own character, for he is a liar and the father of lies" (John 8:44).

The corrupted life produced evil and man became vulnerable to the power of the law of sin and death. The magnitude of this corrupted nature became evident when Cain yielded to evil. It led him to plan and execute the murder of his younger brother, Able.

Before Cain's murderous deed, God said to him in Genesis 4:7, "If you do well, will you not be accepted? And if you do not do well, sin is crouching at the door. Its desire is for you, but you must rule over it." Note that even in the fallen state, God saw something in Cain he could use to rule over sin. How much more the reborn state with Christ's identity.

LESSON: *Sin has an identity, Satan, and he will seek to indwell or influence all who ignore their identity in Christ. You hold the key to either allow or deny sin the opportunity to lead you into the many lifestyles and deeds of the world. Sin always looks for opportunities!*

After Cain murderous deed, sin, and evil increased far beyond imagination as indicated in Genesis Chapter 6. The Lord saw that the wickedness of man was great in the earth, and that every intention of the thoughts of his heart was only evil continually. The Lord was sorry that He had made man on the earth, and it grieved Him to His heart. Therefore, God said, "I will blot out man whom I have created from the face of the land, man and animals and creeping things and birds of the heavens, for I am sorry that I have made them" (Genesis 6:5-7). True to His word, God wiped men from the face of the earth with a flood but saved Noah and his family, eight people.

The Restoration of Identity (God's DNA)

After the intrusion of the corrupted DNA from Satan, wickedness grew with uncontrollable proportions. Even after the floods of Noah's time, evil and wickedness grew, leading men and women to increased levels of sin.

LESSON: *Do not underestimate the power of sin, evil, and wickedness. Stay in Jesus, for He is your only shield against evil.*

Today, there is good news! God has accomplished the redemption of man through Jesus Christ. By Jesus, men, women, and children receive the restoration of God's DNA through their born-again experience and through water baptism.

The Bible says in Romans 6:3-4, "Do you not know that as many of us as were baptized into Jesus Christ were baptized into His death? Therefore we were buried with Him by baptism into death, so that as Christ was raised up from the dead by the glory of the Father; even so we also should walk in newness of life."

Spiritual Identity

Today, history identifies Moses as the deliverer of the children of Israel from the land of ancient Egypt. Moses did not claim himself a deliverer. The King of Heaven chose him and made him so. Joseph did not claim he was the deliverer of his family in the time of famine, which eventually brought the family to ancient Egypt. The King of Heaven made him so. David did not pride himself as the one who could take down the Philistine giant to deliver the armies of Israel from the Philistines. The King of Heaven prepared him behind the scenes to give him confidence to declare himself one who could.

LESSON: *In the spiritual realm, you can only claim to be what the King of Heaven defines you or sees you. No one can define you and you cannot use an outward show or make-believe to define or fake who you are! You are who you are truly in the eyes of God and you are due only what you deserve.*

The King of Heaven has declared you as a new creation with the identity of His son, Jesus Christ. Heaven sees you as an earthen-vessel with the power of Heaven in you. Now, God is in the process of conforming you to the glory and the image of His son.

LESSON: *The way Heaven sees you comes with certain benefits, or lack thereof. These benefits have influence on your life both on the natural and spiritual levels.*

The Bible calls on you to set your mind on things that are above, not on things that are on the earth. It says you have died, and God has hidden you with Christ in God. When Christ (who is your life) appears, then you also will appear with Him in glory (Colossians 3:2-4). It is like three concentric circles, one within the other. You are the innermost circle.

How did you die? Initially, you die when you genuinely repent of your sins. After death, comes burial, which your baptism represents. Repentance before baptism makes your baptism genuine. Godly sorrow proves genuine repentance (2 Corinthians 7:10)! Because your baptism is genuine, the Spirit of God identifies you with the death of Jesus Christ. In fact, all who baptize into Christ Jesus are buried with Him (Colossians 2:12). In genuine baptism, spiritual death and resurrection occur (Colossians 2:11-13). Consequently, God forgives all your trespasses and He sees you as a new spiritual being and He raises you up supernaturally and seats you with Christ in heavenly places.

The Bible says in Ephesians 2:4-6, "But God, being rich in mercy, because of the great love with which He loved us, even when we were dead in our trespasses, made us alive together with Christ—by grace you have been saved—and raised us up with Him and seated us with Him in the heavenly places in Christ Jesus."

Though nothing has changed on the physical level, but because God calls those things that are not as though they are, He sees you as righteous, holy, truthful, and a person of integrity. You are no longer who you used to be, but you are now a new creation. Therefore, acknowledge your position in Christ, who sits at God's right hand.

Now, what is there "above", as referenced in Colossians 3:2, that God calls you to set your mind on? It is your new self, your new identity in Christ. Your new self is precious, like a treasure, and God wants you to keep always pure, no matter your age, as a Christian. Normally, things done repeatedly for a long time become common to the senses. Do not let your new self or identity become common in your senses.

If you view your new self as treasure, your heart will follow. Jesus said where your treasure is, there your heart will be also (Matthew 6:21). In addition, the command to set your mind on things above is a call to live the Christian life with kingdom-oriented thinking. The power of your identity comes to you after Jesus baptizes you with the Holy Spirit and fire.

Below, I have list the attributes of your new identity in Christ, with some associated benefits as indicated in God's Word.

I. You are made anew in the likeness of God with true righteousness and holiness—Ephesians 4:24.

    a. Positioned with Christ at the right hand of God—Colossians 3:1.

    b. Have the righteousness, sanctification, redemption, and wisdom of God through Christ—1 Corinthians 1:30.

    c. Washed by the blood of Jesus Christ, sanctified and justified in His name—1 Corinthians 6:11.

    d. Delivered and translated from the power of darkness to the Kingdom of Christ—Colossians 1:13.

    e. Blessed in Christ with every spiritual blessing in the heavenly places—Ephesians 1:3.

    f. God has chosen you as a part of a royal priesthood and a holy nation, and God's own possession—1 Peter 2:9.

Through your repentance and baptism in Jesus, your old nature dies. You are born again not by the perishable seed of the first Adam, but by the imperishable seed of the Last Adam, Jesus Christ, the living and abiding Word of God (1 Peter 1:23). Since death occurred and a new birth took place, it restores God's DNA to a newly born child of God. The new birth restores man's spiritual significance in relation to God. This restoration will climax in those who identify their new status in Christ and choose to suffer with Him. They will be glorified with Him (Romans 8:17).

The journey from your new birth to the climax of your spiritual significance in Christ in Heaven is compared with Israel's journey and experiences from the Red Sea to the Promised Land (1 Corinthians 10:1-13). They all received baptism into Moses in the Red Sea and in the cloud that followed them. For many of them, God was not pleased and therefore, He overthrew them in the wilderness. Today, the Bible says it is possible to experience a cutting off if you fail to live in God's kindness (Romans 11:21-22).

Therefore, let the restoration of God's DNA to you motivate your daily life and lifestyle. Desire to want to live and walk in the benefits it brings to you through Christ Jesus' redemptive work. He wants you to die daily to worldly and fleshly enticements that could take your heart and mind out of God's purposes for your life.

God has justified you by His grace as a gift and He wants you to live for Him through His son, Christ Jesus. However, you do not see God or Jesus in His physical form. Nevertheless, you see His word. Since God and His word are the same, learning to live for God is to learn to define your daily life issues and experiences by His word. There is no place in the Christian growth process, where someone can say, "I am done with walking by God's Word". Walking by God's Word is an everlasting calling.

LESSON: *The proof of belief and love of God is your obedience to His Word. Lack of obedience to God's Word is unbelief. Remember, Jesus obeyed His Father to the "least" Word.*

In death and resurrection through baptism, God spiritually raised you up with Jesus Christ and seated you with Himself in the heavenly places. This is your place as a born-again, spirit-filled child of God. He wants you to live in this place so He will show you His immeasurable grace in kindness to you in Christ Jesus.

Jesus died that He might redeem you from slavery to lawlessness in this world. You do not have to be a part of the lifestyle from which God has redeemed you. In baptism, you died with Christ Jesus, and spiritually you resurrected to a new life. Though the old self and its ways still exist in the world, God sees them as dead in your life in Christ. If God sees them as dead, you also have to acknowledge them as dead and no longer a part of you.

In baptism, your spirit appeals to God for a good conscience, which you will need in order to live the new life in Jesus Christ. A good and clear conscience is required to help you accept God's Word as true and important. It will help you overcome the world's many evil ways you would confront in your journey to your maximized spiritual significance—the glory of Christ Jesus on His return.

LESSON: *Lack of knowledge of God's will and His ways has destroyed hundreds, but the lack of good and clear conscience is destroying thousands. Do not be a victim!*

If you gain an illumination of the awesomeness of your new identity in Christ, it will influence how you live in this corrupt world.

Chapter 3
Call to Pursue the New Identity

The new self in Christ Jesus has the imprint of God, His DNA. God's command to put on your new self is significant. With your understanding of Colossians 3:4, you may ask, "Well, if my new self will automatically come with Christ when He appears, why the command to put it on now?" If you have a new self, positioned with Christ in God, and God's command is to put on the new self, it is an indication that God expects one or all of the following, concerning you and your new self:

- That your conduct in life will approach the attributes of His nature ascribed to you in your new self, and positioned with Christ in God. God knows all things. He will complete His work in you. However, He knows those who are serious about their salvation and those who love both the world and Christ.
- That you would use God's grace to refuse the world transforming and conforming you to her attributes or mold.

Recall that Apostle Peter counsels you to live a fruitful Christian life so you would not fall (2Peter 1:5-10). In addition, the Bible calls on you to learn endurance and a life of faith because the beast will receive the authority to make war on the Saints and overcome them. The beast cannot overcome you if you have built your foundation on the power of your identity in Christ and your faith in Him is solid. Otherwise, the beast will have authority to tear you down from your high place in heaven (Revelation 13:7-10). Your new self in experience is growing towards your positional nature in Christ.

God's command to put on your new self, your identity in Christ is part of the calling to work out your salvation. What does it mean to work out your salvation? From the passage in Ephesians 4:22-24, you will find the following (and many other subsets) that constitute working out your salvation:

- Put off the old self with its attitudes, mindset, and lifestyles. To do so, you have to subscribe to the life of the Spirit through obedience to God's Word.
- Be renewed in the spirit of your mind, which helps make your mind spiritual to understand the will of the God, who is Spirit.
- To put on the attitudes and lifestyle of the real you in Christ, the new you has a nature like God, righteousness and holiness.

These three bullet points may seem very simple on paper. However, they constitute the demand of your salvation and the Christian warfare, which Christ wants you to win for Him to crown you as a conqueror and a place on His throne. Learn to put on the full armor of God to help you overcome the forces in world, the flesh, and to be protected from your spiritual enemies.

You are working out something for your tomorrow's glory. It is therefore very important to take heed to the command to work out your salvation. Your daily life issues come with challenges in your relationships. However, if you draw from the divine power of God available to you, you will gain the ability to practice the attributes of your identity despite the corruption in the world.

You cannot claim Christ's righteousness and holiness and continue to yield to corruption in this world. That will be a presumptuous and deceptive Christian lifestyle. Do not presume the attributes God has assigned to your new self (identity), positioned in Christ, and ignore God's command to practice these attributes in your life experiences. The Bible says in 1 John 2:6, "He who says he abides in Him ought himself also to walk even as He walked." Again, in 1 John 2:29, the Bible says, "If you know that He is righteous, you know that everyone who practices righteousness is born of Him."

Whoever is in Christ is a new creation. The new creation has the attributes of the likeness of Jesus Christ, which consists of righteousness, godliness, and holiness. This is the sum total of your new self, identity, and positioned with Christ Jesus in God. Therefore, you are a new creation but you will agree with me that sometimes, on the natural level, your mindset, different attitudes, and lifestyle do not always reflect your newness.

LESSON: *Learn to live your new life in Jesus so that when all the "churchy" things you do end, you will have something built up in your inner life, which you can present to God as a sacrifice.*

Remember that God calls those things that are not as though they were. Therefore, God sees you as a new creation and you have to acknowledge the identity He has given you in Christ. Seek grace to help you live a life that daily grows you in the attributes of your new creation, the new self or identity in Christ. God calls on you to lay aside sin and anything that will weigh you down in this Christian race. God wants you to see to it that you do not fail to obtain His grace, and that no "root of bitterness" springs up in you to defile you (Hebrews 12:15).

He wants you to look to Jesus who is the author and finisher of your faith. God wants you to learn from Jesus, who for the joy that was set before Him endured the cross, despising the shame, and is now seated at the right hand of the throne of God (Hebrews 12:2). He alone is the source of your new identity, and helps to complete your transformation. He is going to spew out those who are not serious with the Christian life.

The attributes of the new identity consist of a lifestyle every believer has to choose. Any worldly lifestyle will limit or diminish the manifestation of the power of your new identity in Christ. Therefore, God commands you to put on or practice your new self. This is how God, as you allow Him, will mold your personality change into the person positioned with Christ in God.

The call to put on the new self (the new identity) is a critical calling. This is a call that will mature you in some critical areas of your new creation. In order to put on the new self, new creation or you new identity, the old self must go—"Put off, concerning the former conduct, the old man, which grows corrupt according to the deceitful lusts".

For the new self to take root and manifest in your daily life, your mind requires renewal to help increase your knowledge regarding the will of God. It is a life-long process to keep renewing your mind. Your renewed mind will help you discover God's will so you will learn to walk in the attributes of godliness, righteousness, and holiness. Jesus walked the earth as God's son and in power according to the Spirit of Holiness (Romans 1:4).

The new identity in Christ is your new creation, which has to grow in an increasing measure towards maturity. Christ has therefore become your new life and there is no other way you can live but through Him. When you grow in the attributes of your identity in Christ, you grow toward the full measure of your new creation in Him. This is awesome to know! However, it places a demand on you daily to consecrate yourself. Walk in the power of the Holy Spirit so you can fulfill God's purposes for you in this life.

If you live a faithful life to God, your light will shine with the glory of Christ wherever God places you in this world. It brings glory to the Father. Therefore, as you have received Christ Jesus the Lord, so walk in Him, rooted, built up in Him, established in the faith, and abounding in thanksgiving.

God has destined you not only to attain intellectual proficiency in His Word; He also wants you to manifest His kingdom character and power, which are the attributes of your new identity in Christ. He wants to clothe you with the glory of Christ Jesus when He returns.

Example of Priming a Water Pump

In one of my evangelistic missions to Africa, I had the opportunity to live for a few days in the mission house belonging to Manna Mission. One morning I went to the kitchen to prepare my morning tea. I turned on the faucet and there was no water. Meanwhile, I had seen the keeper of the place turn on a switch whenever we ran out of water. Since I could not find the keeper, I went to the room where the pump was, and turned on the switch just as I previously saw the keeper do. Unfortunately, the pump gave a very loud screeching sound. I turned off the switch and waited for the keeper.

Fortunately, the keeper showed up after just ten minutes. I told him what happened and he showed me a bottle of water he uses to prime the pump. That was very interesting! He poured a little water into the body of the pump and that helped it to pump more water high into a poly-tank located at the top of the roof of the building.

God has "primed" you with the righteousness, holiness, and godliness of Jesus Christ. He expects you to move higher up the Heavenly call upon your life. He wants you to produce or "pump out" more of these characteristics in your daily life issues. You see, when the poly-tank on the roof was filling up, the water in the kitchen started to flow and I was able to prepare my morning tea. When you walk in the attributes of your new self in Christ, your life produces what other people need for their difficult and broken lives. They are satisfied when their lives intersect yours. That shows who you are becoming—an heir to Christ's Kingdom who will have compassion regarding people's needs.

Your understanding of the priming of a pump will help you understand the imputed attributes God has given you in Christ. For example, you have the righteousness, holiness, and godliness of Christ, but God commands you to put them on. The water used to prime a water pump is not what the owner expects from the pump. The owner expects the pump to use the water it received to provide more water for the benefit of providing hydration for the people in the community. You have to use the righteousness of Christ imputed to you to produce a life of righteousness for the sake of people. Jesus prayed to God in John 17:19 (KJV), "And for their sakes I sanctify myself, that they also might be sanctified through the truth".

Because you allow God to train you in the Word of righteousness, it makes you skillful in the practice of righteousness as a lifestyle. It also exercises or trains your conscience to differentiate between right and wrong (Hebrews 5:13-14). Learn to endure suffering that comes with your practice of righteousness because Kingdom rulers do not switch to unrighteousness in their times of difficulties. You are a ruler in the making! Learn stability and self-control in your emotional life and remain faithful to the Lord through all that the world throws at you.

LESSON: *If you are a person who desires that people treat you well, according to the Scriptures, you may not be able to endure suffering or persecution.*

You have to learn to take up the whole armor of God, that you may be able to withstand in the evil days, and having done all, to stand firm and faithful to your Redeemer (Ephesians 6:13). Jesus suffered many of the things you and I go through in this world, even all that Satan threw at Him, but He remained faithful to His God. This shows the heart of a ruler. The Bible says Jesus learned obedience by the things He suffered, which perfected Him and He became the source of eternal salvation for all who obey Him (Hebrews 5:8-9).

Writing to the believers in Galatia, Apostle Paul said you are the son of God. Because you are a son, you are an heir of God through Christ (Galatians 4:6-7). You are going to reign with Christ. Therefore, you have to learn some lifestyles, including the following:

- Learn to use God's grace effectively. Romans 5:21 says, "So that, as sin has reigned in death, grace also might reign through righteousness leading to eternal life through Jesus Christ our Lord". The kingdom of a king is established through righteousness (Proverbs 16:12). You will please King Jesus because you practice righteousness.
- Grow the mind of Christ within you by humbling your heart to His Word.
- Learn and understand righteousness, truth, justice, mercy, and holiness. Because you are going to rule over the unrighteous, you have to rule over unrighteousness in your life now.
- Learn endurance and self-control in your life issues. God is grooming sons who have self-control, so they will not use His power and authority to harm others unjustly. The son of a king inherits the father's possession. However, he has to endure guidance, training, and necessary disciplines so he can reign on the father's throne.
- Learn to live and walk by the Holy Spirit and be led by Him. This is how sons who will rule with Christ live. They overcome the law

of sin and death with the more powerful law in Christ, the law of the Spirit of Life.

One of the weapons Apostle Paul used to conquer many of his life difficulties and challenges was righteousness, for his right and left hand. This means Apostle Paul lived His Christian life with Kingdom mindedness. In his life issues, Paul practiced righteousness. Righteousness grows through a life of obedience to God. To reign with Christ on His throne, you have to learn endurance. That way you can remain true to God no matter how the world presses on your integrity to live otherwise. The power of grace, even God's Spirit, will help you conquer in this evil world. You are a soon-coming ruler—a co-heir with Christ Jesus.

Therefore, lift up your chest and let the attributes of your new self, shine through your daily lifestyle. Among many other reasons why God commands you to put on the new self or your new identity in Christ, I will consider a few in the next chapter.

Chapter 4
Some Reasons for God's Command to Put on the New Identity in Christ

God's command to you is clear, put on whom He has made you in Christ Jesus. It is a call to practice godliness, righteousness, and holiness in all your life issues. God does nothing in your life except to for a reason, to accomplish His divine purpose for you. Among many other reasons for God's command, I will list and expound upon six in this chapter.

Reason # 1: A Spiritual "Garment" You Keep Pure

God desire is to perfect you through His son, Jesus Christ. He wants you to attain to the fullness of the glory of His son when He appears. Today, He commands you to put on the attributes of who you have become in Christ, your identity. That is, He is giving you the opportunity to desire the level of glory you want to appear when you come with Christ. Your new self is a spiritual garment or clothing reserved for you in Heaven. While you live in this world, your life confronts challenges, difficulties, temptations, evils, and even persecutions. However, you have the opportunity to choose how to handle these life issues by using the grace God has given.

Your faithfulness and diligence in the pursuit of the attributes of your new self (identity) in Christ against the challenges of life will define the purity of your new self, your garment. As you learn to practice your new self, your identity, it becomes a part of your life. Keeping or maintaining the purity of your new self maintains your place in Christ. You do this through faith and the power of God's Spirit, whom He has shed upon us abundantly, and His grace (Titus 3:5-6, Titus 2:12-13).

As you apply and obey God's Word, it keeps you from ungodliness, unrighteousness, unholy attitudes, behaviors, and various lusts that plague the world. God wants you to deny and overcome corruption. Your victory over corruption builds God's divine nature in you, which is your true nature in Christ (2 Peter 1:4). Your lifestyles and deeds after your new birth are critical and affect your spiritual garment. It either can introduce blemishes and soil in your garment, or will keep it purified.

Apostle Paul said he died daily. To die daily is to identify and genuinely repent from deeds, attitudes, and lifestyles that could corrupt your body and spirit all over again. The Holy Spirit is the help you have to do this. The deeds of the flesh diminish your ability to keep pure the garment of your new self. The desires of the flesh are opposed to the desires of the Spirit of God in you.

The deeds of the flesh produce spiritual death points, which diminish your spiritual strength and status in Christ. If fleshly deeds persist, it eventually leads to spiritual death. Therefore, use God's grace to overcome and grow out of a fleshly mentality. A fleshly mentality always leads to fleshly deeds, which soils the garment of your new self in Christ. The Bible says in Romans 8:12, "Therefore, brethren, we are debtors, not to the flesh, to live after the flesh."

Understand the call to live by the Spirit. This is how you can build deep solid roots in Jesus Christ, which keeps you out of condemnation (Romans 8:1). In Christ, you have the Law of the Spirit of life to keep the garment of your new self continually washed in the blood of Jesus.

Your life in Christ, the new self, enlarges as you learn to live and walk by the Spirit. If you are submissive and diligent in the practice of your new self, the power of the Holy Spirit helps you overcome weaknesses due to the flesh. He helps you also overcome corruptible ways that plague many in this world. The Holy Spirit will lead you in the paths of righteousness for His name's sake.

The Bible says in Revelation 7:14, "These are the ones coming out of the great tribulation. They have washed their robes and made them white in the blood of the Lamb." No matter what you go through in this life, God expects you to practice who you are in Christ. That way, you will keep your garment pure and not yield to intentional sinning (Hebrews 9:7; 10:26). Intentional sinning is to know and understand the truths of God's word but ignore it for your own wicked will.

If the Spirit of Him who raised Jesus from the dead dwells in you, He will also give life to your mortal bodies through His Spirit who dwells in you (Romans 8:11). Consequently, you will not continue to live according to the dictates of your weak flesh, which can lead you into sinful ways.

When Christ appears, you will appear with Him in your garment, soiled or unsoiled. Therefore, you have to heed 1 John 3:3, to purify your life in today's world so you will keep your garment always pure and not soiled by sin, wickedness, and evil ways. Your Christian calling is to learn to live a godly and righteous holy life. The angel of the Lord said to the angel of the church of Sardis, "Yet you have still a few names in Sardis, people who have not soiled their garments, and they will walk with Me in white, for they are worthy" (Revelation 3:4).

The angel of the Lord said in Revelation 16:15, "Behold, I am coming as a thief. Blessed is he who watches, and keeps his garments, lest he walks naked, and they see his shame (KJV)."

You may ask, "What is this garment?" The garment represents your new identity (new self) seated with Christ in the heavenly places. A soiled garment represents a loss of your spiritual significance, the identity, new self in Christ; consequently, you will not be clothed enough to take away or cover your shame. Your spiritual significance is God's gift of godliness, righteousness, and holiness, found in your new self.

Apostle Paul said in 2 Corinthians 5:1-4 (KJV), "For we know that if our earthly house of this tabernacle were dissolved, we have a building of God, an house not made with hands, eternal in the heavens. For in this we groan, earnestly desiring to be clothed upon with our house, which is from heaven: If so be that being clothed we shall not be found naked. For we that are in this tabernacle do groan, being burdened: not for that we would be unclothed, but clothed upon, that mortality might be swallowed up of life." The Bible also says, "For as in Adam all die, even so in Christ all shall be made alive. But each one in his own order: Christ the first fruits; afterward those who are Christ's at His coming" (1 Corinthians 15:22-23).

God is going to reward your diligence with the glory appropriate with how you have kept the garment of your new self. This is how some people, especially Christians, would either embrace the dazzling brightness of the returning Christ or shrink from Him in fear. First John 2:28 (KJV) says, "And now, little children, abide in him; that, when he shall appear, we may have confidence, and not be ashamed before him at his coming". Because you keep your spiritual garment pure, you will not shrink from Jesus in shame when He returns.

Reason # 2: A Closer Relationship with God

A closer relationship with God enhances your participation in God's divine nature. The fact that a person has an identity in Christ does not necessarily imply that one is walking in the attributes of that identity. On the other hand, God's desire is a deeper intimate relationship with you. For this reason, He says to you to practice the attributes of your new self because the new self is the divine nature of Christ who lives in the center of God. Therefore, the practice of your new self brings you closer to God. It brings you into a deeper intimate relationship with Him.

The practice of godliness, righteousness, and holiness helps you deny ungodliness and worldly lusts. Worldly lusts are what introduce corruption or blemishes in people's lives again. Because you deny ungodliness and worldly lusts, you come to participate in the divine nature of God (2 Peter 1:4). Participation in the divine nature of God introduces you to the power of creative words. God takes delight that you walk in this lifestyle. You are able to speak creative words into your own life situations and into the life of others.

Jesus said in Revelation 3:20 (KJV), "Behold, I stand at the door, and knock: if any man hears My voice, and opens the door, I will come in to him, and will sup with him, and he with Me." To open the door to Christ happens through a conscious life of obedience to His Word. He said in John 14:23 (KJV), "If a man loves Me, he will keep My words: and My Father will love him, and We will come unto him, and make our abode with him."

To abide in Him, and He in you is intimacy at the spiritual level. When Apostle Paul tasted the closeness with Christ, he said in Philippians 3:8-9a (KJV), "Yea doubtless, and I count all things but loss for the excellency of the knowledge of Christ Jesus my Lord: for whom I have suffered the loss of all things, and do count them but dung, that I may win Christ, and be found in Him." Therefore, your diligent pursuit of the attributes of your new self will bring you closer and into a deeper relationship with Christ.

Reason # 3: The Full Measure and Stature as a Son

The Bible says in John 1:12, "But as many as received Him, to them gave He power to become the sons of God, even to them that believe on His name". It is important to pay attention to the phrase, "...gave He power to become the sons of God". Because you have received or believed on Jesus, God has predestined you to be conformed to the image of your Savior, Jesus Christ (Romans 8:29).

God has given you the power to attain to this destiny. It is the earnest expectation of Heaven and Earth. The Bible says creation waits with eager longing for the manifestation of the sons of God (Romans 8:19). The creation is waiting on you to yield to the leading of God's Holy Spirit, to help you put on your new self. In the process, you become conformed to the Son of God. All who are led by the Spirit of God are sons of God (Romans 8:14).

What is Heaven's expectation for you? Heaven wants you to put away all malice and deceit, and any root of bitterness, hypocrisy, envy, and slander. Like newborn infants, God wants you to long for the pure spiritual milk (His Word), that by it, you may grow up into salvation, if indeed, you have tasted the goodness of the Lord (1 Peter 2:2-3). The Word must be pure. That means gaining comprehension of the Word in its correct context and not redefining it to justify the way you want to live or what you want to do.

LESSON: *It is not the number of years you have been a Christian that qualifies you as a son. It is learning to live by God's Spirit and putting off fleshly, childish deeds. It is possible to hold some type of leadership role such as a bishop, apostle, pastor, prophet or an evangelist, and yet still be an infant.*

You are as an infant if you inordinately crave for worldly and fleshly things instead of things directed by the Holy Spirit. When you grow up or are growing up into a son, your focus become increasingly Kingdom oriented. You gain control over worldly and fleshly distractions that come to compete with your significance in the Lord. Learn to focus on God. He supplies all your needs according to His riches in glory by Christ Jesus (Philippians 4:19).

God wants you to become spiritually mature through the practice of His Word of love. This is how you can live and walk like a son and not an infant. You will gain the ability to renew your mind to help you know God by revelation. You gain the ability to discern His will; hence, you will have the power to distinguish right from wrong in your life issues. Anyone who struggles with righteousness is unskilled in the matters of the Kingdom of Christ.

The mature or maturing sons of God learn to distinguish righteousness from unrighteousness and between what is good and what is evil. Therefore, they expand their walk in the attributes of their new identity in Christ.

The immature sons need someone to take care of them. The Psalmist says God will instruct you and teach you in the way you should go. He will counsel you with His eye upon you. Therefore, be not like a horse or a mule, without understanding, which must be curbed with bit and bridle, or it will not stay near to you (Psalm 32:8-9).

Do you have enough of God's Word in you to help you withstand the temptation to switch to fleshly deeds when there is no one around to hold you accountable? God calls on you to work out your own salvation. You do so not because a pastor, a deacon, or a Christian Brother or sister is with you. God wants you to learn to do so much more in the absence of everyone else and when no one is looking over your shoulders (Philippians 2:12). You do so in the fear of God and in trembling.

Apostle Paul said when he was a child, he spoke like a child; he thought like a child, he reasoned like a child. When he became a man, he gave up childish ways (1 Corinthians 13:11). Do you still think and behave like an infant in your Christian life? Because he was maturing, Apostle Paul said he did not live his Christian life carelessly as a boxer who beats the air. Rather, he disciplined his body and kept it under control so he would not be disqualified after preaching the Gospel to many (1 Corinthians 9:27).

If you have been a Christian for a while and still struggle with the flesh and worldliness, it is an indication that you are still an infant and need to grow up. It is very important to take note of Paul's statement in 1 Corinthians 9:27. Many Christians presume a glorious status in Heaven irrespective of how they live after salvation. Paul's attitude in his Christian life is typical of a believer who truly understands the heavenly calling and who yields to God's conforming processes.

Apostle Paul's love for Christ controlled him, because he came to understand that Christ died for all, that those who live might no longer live for themselves but for Him who for their sake died and was raised (2 Corinthians 5:14-15). Paul understood and gained an accurate knowledge of his relationship with Christ Jesus. To live for the Lord and not for self is a doorway to Christian maturity. To help you grow into a mature son, take note of the following:

- Sons of God learn to fight their spiritual battles without yielding to compromise and unfaithfulness to God. They understand truth, humility, righteousness, godliness, holiness, and the call to live by the Spirit.
- The sons of God are those who yield to the leading of His Spirit. You have to learn the Holy Spirit-led life in your daily life issues. To do so, you have to learn some things:

  o Do not cloud your mind and heart with inordinate cares for the things of life.
  o You have to be a person of much prayer.
  o You have to learn to yield your heart to righteousness, justice, love, godliness, truth, godly fear, and the things that promote holiness.

o   The Word of Christ must dwell in you richly, which orients your heart spiritually to discern the voice of the Holy Spirit from the many voices in the world.

o   Do not allow the flesh to make you a person with many careless words. It makes you fleshly, which will open you up for unfruitful and untrue words. The fleshly mind cannot comprehend the things of the Spirit, let alone be led by Him.

Because you yield to these lifestyles and others, God's grace helps you put to death the deeds of the old self. Then your conformation into a son of God will accelerate. Jesus said His sheep hear His voice and they follow Him and He knows them. As you grow into a son, the voice of Jesus comes to you in distinct ways through His Spirit. Take delight and cooperate with God's plan to grow you into a son and a part of His special people.

Reason # 4: To Reign with Christ

The Kingdom of Christ is not going to be like anything you and I have ever seen or know in this world. The symbol of power and authority of His Kingdom is righteousness. It is going to be an everlasting Kingdom of absolute righteousness. If you fail to mature in the walk of righteousness, which is one of the attributes of your new identity, you cannot become joint heir to the throne of Jesus.

The Bible says in Hebrews1:8 (KJV), "Your throne, O God, is forever and ever, the scepter of uprightness is the scepter of your kingdom." God is grooming you to become join-heir to the throne in Christ. Romans 8:16-17 says, "The Spirit Himself bears witness with our spirit that we are children of God, and if children, then heirs-heirs of God and fellow heirs with Christ, provided we suffer with Him in order that we may also be glorified with Him."

In which way do you suffer with Christ? Learn to endure all that the world throws at you and keep yourself from anything that could corrupt your life, no matter how appealing. The Bible says in Psalm 34:19, "Many are the afflictions of the righteous, but the Lord delivers him out of them all".

When you make up your mind to live your new identity in Christ, you will encounter difficulties. Nevertheless, your new lifestyle leads to life. Suffering also includes your ability to endure God's work that takes you from your day of redemption to your status as a son. Remember that what

Joseph went through in God's hands took him from the day of promise to his greatness in ancient Egypt.

Jesus said in Revelation 3:21, "To him who overcomes I will grant to sit with Me in My throne, as I also overcame, sat down with My Father on His throne." You conquer the enticements of the world, of the flesh, and of demonic spirits who seek to manipulate your mind to deviate from righteousness. The effective way to conquer in this evil age is to practice the attributes of your new identity in Christ. You are going to reign with Christ in His Kingdom of righteousness. So pay attention to the key phrases in the above passages, "…provided you suffer with Him" and "…the one who conquers".

How do you conquer? Irrespective of what goes on in this world and the rampant lifestyle of self and evil, you can conquer. Learn to define your daily lifestyle by the demands that the attributes of your new self places on your life. The will of God for you is that you will not become a Christian who ignores His command but to put on your new identity in Christ.

LESSON: *Do not become one of those who claim to have the righteousness of Christ but fail to practice their claim.*

That should not be you! You know the power God has invested in you through the attributes of your new self in Christ. You are diligent in your walk in these attributes. You know God wants you to grow your skills in the Word of righteousness. You know and understand that God is taking you through skills training, to produce in you the divine attributes that will qualify you as a ruler.

I believe Jesus is looking for mayors, governors, kings, and priests to rule with Him on His throne. For this reason, learn to endure all of God's disciplines that could come in your life to make you into a real ruler. Walk in godly fear because God gets involved in your training! Learn endurance; it will help you endure every discipline you go through at God's hands.

God's disciplines may sometimes seem painful rather than pleasant at this moment, but later it yields the peaceful fruit of righteousness. It gets your soul, spirit, and body in shape to share His holiness (Hebrews 12:10-11), which are the qualities of a Kingdom ruler. The mistake you could make is neglecting to catch the purpose of God's disciplines. Do not allow the flesh to cause you to take a detour from the path of righteousness because you could not endure God's chastening.

As a Christian destines to rule with Christ, never fail to discover or understand God's demand for righteousness, holiness, and godliness in your daily life issues. Do not let down your strong confidence in God's plans for you now and for the future. Then you can endure all that God takes you through to make you a real son, a priest, and a ruler. Remember…if Jesus had let down in His daily practice of righteousness, He would have failed in God's purpose to make Him the author of your salvation or take on the title, "King of kings and Lord of lords!" Jesus was righteous, yet, His love for righteousness and hatred of wickedness earned Him God's anointing and elevation far beyond His companions.

LESSON: *In the eyes of the King of Heaven, what is wickedness? A life of wickedness is to know what will honor God but refuse to honor Him in your life issues.*

Reason # 5: Victory over Sin

You cannot claim to have God's likeness, righteousness, and holiness and continue to yield to corruption in this world. First John 3:7 says, "Little children, let no one deceive you. Whoever practices righteousness is righteous, as He is righteous." Your identity in Christ comes with enough power to overcome presumptuous and deceptive thinking. Do not presume the attributes of your identity in Christ and ignore God's command to practice these attributes.

First John 3:9 (KJV) says, "Whosoever is born of God doth not commit sin; for his seed remaineth in him: and he cannot sin, because he is born of God". Again, in 1 John 5:18 the Bible says, "We know that whoever is born of God does not sin; but he who has been born of God keeps himself, and the wicked one does not touch him."

The key to the assertion in 1 John 3:9 and 1 John 5:18 is the godly nature of your new identity in Christ. God's goal for you is the formation of Christ in you, which provides your victory over sin because the Christ nature or godly nature cannot sin. Your baptism and the provision of grace makes it possible for you to do God's will through Christ. You respond correctly to God's Word in life issues, and you overcome corruption, which opens you up to participate in God's divine nature. The godly nature is the Christ nature and it cannot sin because it is the nature of God.

God's command to practice your new nature in this corrupt world activates the Christian warfare. You have to fight daily to maintain your status in Christ. There are spiritual and worldly forces, even your flesh that works hard to prevent you from obeying God's command. To help you do what He commands, God has given you abundance of His grace. Because you are serious about your new identity in Christ, the grace of God helps you grow in Kingdom mindedness. In fact, Kingdom mindedness enhances the mind and wisdom of Christ in you. With the mind of Christ, you will delight in godliness, holiness, and righteousness in your life issues.

LESSON: *The many fleshly problems in the life of some Christians are the result of an inability or unwillingness to obey God's command to practice the godly nature of their new self. Oftentimes, some are ignorant of the demand to submit to the disciplines of the new self.*

As you mature in the practice of your godly nature, there comes a time when you cease or overcome the inclination to sin. You overcome the sin consciousness. Romans 6:1 say this, "What shall we say then? Are we to continue in sin that grace may abound?" The answer is, "By no means!" God calls on His people to awake to righteousness and cease sinning because some have no knowledge of God's provision for victory over sin (1 Corinthians 15:34). God sees you as a winner through Christ! So see yourself as such and walk as a winner.

Daily you expand your understanding of your new godly nature. You make room to grow your practice of this nature. This is why, in your pursuit of the Kingdom of Christ, you do not entirely set your focus on what you do in church, but more so on what your nature is conforming to. Bad nature corrupts your spirit. Let God's ability help you to overcome sin. For God's ability to work for you, ask yourself if the following are working in your inner self:

- You have an earnest inner desire to work out your salvation—striving daily to practice your new self.
- You have an earnest inner love for God through a life of obedience.
- You have an earnest inner hate for wickedness.

In His life, Jesus chose to hate the sin of wickedness. He chose the love for righteousness through a life of obedience to His Father. He chose God's divine purposes for His life. Consequently, He overcame every trap of sin and sinful enticements. God created Adam and Eve in His likeness, but unlike Jesus, they disobeyed Him.

As a Christian in this age and time, God has given you the opportunity to know some of the failures of past and present men and women of God. God has also granted you the opportunity to know the mysteries of His Kingdom; therefore, you have all of what it takes to defy sin and overcome it with your new godly nature. Jesus died to redeem us from all lawlessness (Titus 2:14).

Many of the lawless deeds and lifestyle in this world are due to people yielding to forces of the world and of the flesh. Because you learn to overcome the world and the flesh, your life will produce the fruit of the Spirit. It measures your diligence in the Christian life. The fruit of the Spirit measure how much of Christ has formed in you. In addition, God rewards your diligence because you triumph over the world and your flesh.

If God's command is to put on your new self, then He expects your life in this corrupt world to move towards matching your identity in Christ. Oftentimes, you do not know where you are in this journey of putting off the old self. However, if you are paying attention to God's work in you, you may identify where you are by the things that proceed out of you in some of your attitudes in your interpersonal relationships.

LESSON: *When people rock the "boat" of your life through offenses and attitudes, you have to bless them. What they do against you and what comes out of you helps you discover the level you have put off your old self.*

Success in your spiritual growth as a Christian is your ability to reign over the old self with its attitudes and ways. God's command is clear—friendship with the world (old self) is enmity with God (James 4:4). In addition, your level of success as a Christian is in the offering of your body to God as a holy sacrifice, renewing of the spirit of the mind, and growing in the attributes of your new self. This is a delightful life in the eyes of the King of Heaven because it leads to your victory over your old self.

Reason # 6: Part of Christ's Army

The battle today and in the day of Christ's return is the battle of righteousness against unrighteousness. This places a demand on you to take the call to righteousness very seriously. Today, the Bible says that though you live in this physical world, your battle or warfare is not according to the flesh (people). Your daily battles are against rulers, against authorities, and against spiritual forces of evil in the heavenly places. Therefore, the Lord calls on you to be strong and to adorn yourself with His whole armor to protect yourself against the onslaught of the enemies of God.

LESSON: *Any Spirit-filled believer who sees people as the source of his/her problems may probably be lacking in the knowledge of his/her identity in Christ and the demand that comes with it.*

God is conforming you into the image of Jesus Christ, the King of kings and the Lord of lords. The enemies of your identity in Jesus hate your present and future position in Him. They war against you daily for an opportunity to distract your heart so that you will walk or live far less than whom God has ordained you to be in Jesus.

Your daily battle is the battle of righteousness. One of the attributes of your new identity in Christ is righteousness and God commands you to put it on. To put on righteousness is a call to obedience. Romans 6:16 says "Do you not know that if you present yourselves to anyone as obedient slaves, you are slaves of the one whom you obey, either of sin, which leads to death, or of obedience, which leads to righteousness?"

Today, the enemies of your identity war against you through the weaknesses in your flesh, which you fail to bring under subjection to Christ (1 Peter 2:11). Your spiritual enemies seek that you will subscribe to unrighteousness in your daily life issues. However, if you overcome because you put on the entire armor of God, no weapon fashioned against you shall prosper (Isaiah 54:14-17). Christ will qualify you as one of His called and chosen, His own special individual who will be a part of His army in the last days. The enemies of God will make war on the Lamb, and the Lamb will conquer them, for He is Lord of lords and King of kings, and those with Him are called, chosen, and faithful (Revelation 17:14).

The enemies of Christ war against you because you keep God's command and hold on to Christ's testimony (Revelation 12:17). The testimony of Jesus is the Word of prophesy. Apostle Peter said that when they were with Jesus on the mount of transfiguration, they heard the voice of God from heaven. So he says to the church in 2 Peter 1:19, "We also have a more sure Word of prophecy, to which you do well to take heed, as to a light that shines in a dark place, until the day dawns and the Daystar arises in your hearts."

The Daystar, Jesus Christ, will grow in you because you pay attention and live by His Word. You will overcome every weapon the enemy fashions against you and you become the dwelling place of the Lord, not only in today's world but also in the time to come (Isaiah 66:2, Revelation 13:6). You can make yourself a part of the warriors of the Lamb if you learn to grow your skills in the attributes of your new identity. In righteousness, Jesus is going to judge and make war (Revelation 19:11-14).

God has approved that you become clothed with fine linen, bright and pure, which is your life of righteousness (Revelation 19:8). Nevertheless, the choice is yours! Therefore, make yourself available to God today to help you grow in the attributes of your new identity in Christ Jesus. He says that if you overcome, you shall be clothed in white linen (Revelation 3:5). You will become a part of those who follow Jesus, the Lamb of God. The armies in heaven followed Jesus on white horses, clothed in fine linen, white and clean.

Chapter 5

Some Benefits Associated
with Identity in Christ

God is good! He had been this way from the beginning and will be good beyond the end of human time. He said to Apostle John on the Island of Patmos, "I am the Alpha and the Omega," says the Lord God, "who is and who was and who is to come, the Almighty" (Revelation 1:8). He is true and faithful throughout all generations. To help you fulfill His commands, God provides you with help. He provides grace to help you fight the good fight of faith.

God not only provides His grace to help work out your salvation, He also gives you His very exceeding great and precious promises to live by. The Bible says in 2 Peter 1:4, "Whereby are given unto us exceeding great and precious promises: that by these ye might be partakers of the divine nature, having escaped the corruption that is in the world through lust." Below, I will touch on five of the many benefits associated with your new identity in Christ.

1. Knowledge of God

When you gain a revealed knowledge of the Father and the Son, you will discover your identity in Christ in ways that strengthens your belief in Him and His Word. You will gain an understanding of the demand that your identity places on your daily life and lifestyle. You will also discover God has given you power and ability to perform what His Word says about your life in Christ. It is God's creative power and ability residing in your tongue. You will discover that God has subjected all things in the seen and unseen to Jesus, the One in whom you have your identity.

In the power of God's Word, Jesus Christ, all things have their being—they hold together in Him. Even every moment of your life, both the possible and impossible situations, are subject to Jesus. The knowledge of your identity coupled with your inner desire to love both God and people, will help you grow in the knowledge of Him. It grows His fullness in you.

When you know God by revelation through the Spirit of wisdom, you will gain a greater conviction of the reality of His promises. Conviction of God's promises leads to obedience, which produces stability in your Christian experiences. It also increases His presence with you. God has chosen you to know Him; even the mysteries of His Kingdom. He has chosen you, so your lifestyle would shame the wise and strong in the world (1Corinthians 1:26-29).

LESSON: *Do not let the basis of your faith conviction in God's power to help you dwell on the magnitude of your life's situations. Rather, let your faith convictions dwell on God's overwhelming power and ability to redefine your life situation for your victory.*

Your calling in Christ is not dependent on your prestigious position in life or by your influence by the world's standards. Nevertheless, God has chosen you and made you mighty in His kingdom matters. God is sovereign in power and glory, and no man or creature can boast in His presence. Daily, the world sees what you do, but have no idea who you have become. This is so because they do not know Jesus (1 John 3:1b), but you know Him.

God gives you the Spirit of wisdom and of revelation to help you know Him. Jesus said in John 17:3, "And this is eternal life, that they know You the only true God, and Jesus Christ whom You have sent." In His help to bring you to the knowledge of Him, He quickens or enlightens the eyes of your heart so you may know the hope of the inheritance He has in store for you.

God wants you to understand the riches of the glory of His inheritance in the saints. God wants you to know the surpassing greatness of His power at work on your behalf (Ephesians 1:17-19). Knowledge of God and your inner drive to walk in love activate spiritual power because a life of love is a righteous walk. Apostle Paul received God's wisdom to know the mysteries of Christ because of his daily inner-driving desire to see people saved and come to the knowledge of God's grace.

2. Mysteries of Christ's Kingdom

After Jesus told the parable of the seed, His disciples asked Him what the parable meant. Before explaining the meaning of the parable, Jesus said, "To you it is given to know the mysteries of the kingdom of God. But to others I speak in parables, so that seeing they might not see and hearing they might not understand."

Whom did Jesus refer to as "they" in His statement? It is anyone who doubts, ignores, or fails to yield to the Word of God through obedience. If you ignore or doubt God's Word, the Word will become like a parable to your understanding. The understanding that should motivate your obedience will be lost or will not happen for you. This is the reason many people, even some Christians, know the Word of God but fail to apply it in their life issues. They lack the knowledge of God!

3. Ambassador for Christ

Discovery of your identity in Christ will give you the awareness that you are an ambassador for Christ just as He was for God. God was reconciling the world to Himself through Christ, not imputing trespasses to us. Today, God is making His appeal through you and I (2 Corinthians 5:17-20). This makes you an ambassador for Christ.

You are an alien (sojourner or pilgrim) in the world (1 Peter 2:11) and not a citizen. This qualifies believers to assume the ambassadorial status. You live in this world, but you are not of it. Anyone who submit to the worldly lifestyle cannot be the ambassador of Christ

Ambassadors are aliens in the country of their assignment. An ambassador represents his or her country in another. He or she seeks the welfare of His people in the foreign country. Jesus was the ambassador from Heaven who sought the welfare of humanity who has wondered away from the Father. He taught and announced God's goodness and His ways. He brought the good news of God's good intent for humanity. He came to seek and to save the lost (Luke 19:10). He also came to destroy the works of the devil (1 John 3:8). He has assigned to you the same responsibility.

Jesus said in Matthew 28:18-20, "All authority in heaven and on earth has been given to me. Go therefore and make disciples of all nations, baptizing them in the name of the Father and of the Son and of the Holy Spirit, teaching them to observe all that I have commanded you. And behold, I am with you always, to the end of the age."

To accomplish Christ's assignment, you require the ambassadorial authority and the power of your home country-Heaven. You need the Holy Spirit to help you destroy the works of the devil in people's lives. Their freedom helps them hold on to Jesus' teachings and hence, gain the divine strength they need to live as effective ambassadors.

Many Christians stay in church for years and yet they are subject to many wicked works that plague the world; they yield to wicked works of the devil and of the flesh because of their lack of correct orientation to knowledge of the ambassadorial status. As ambassadors of Christ, you have the same dynamic power of the early disciples. All you need to help you function as an effective ambassador is a correct orientation to who you are in Christ.

Jesus came as part of our humanity, to seek and to save the lost. The Bible says He came to His own, and His own people did not receive Him. But to all who did receive Him, who believed in His name, He gave the right to become children of God. These were people born neither of blood, nor by the natural process of birth, nor by the will of man, but of God (John 1:11-13).

As ambassador for Christ, you desire to accomplish the affairs of Heaven for people in this world. Whenever any social or political issue arises, your first line of action is to contact your home country (Heaven) for directives. This was the mode of operation of Jesus Christ when He was here with us in the flesh. He would pray to God with loud cries and supplications (Hebrews 5:7).

As an ambassador for Christ in this world, learn to commune constantly to your headquarters (Heaven), with God through your High Priest, Jesus Christ. Because you have to be an effective ambassador, learn to be a person of much prayer. Your effectiveness as ambassador diminishes if you lack much prayer in your life.

LESSON: *A person's approach to life issues and situations usually defines the inner content of that person.*

As an ambassador of Heaven, approach life and define life issues and situations by the policies of Heaven, which dwell within you. What dwells in you is the Word of God. True knowledge and submission to the demands of the identity in Christ will empower your ambassadorial status in this world.

LESSON: *The greatness of your identity in Christ is not just in the abundance of knowledge you have of the "policies" of Heaven (the word of God), but more so, in the degree the policies are conforming you to the attributes of your identity in Him. In this is the authority and the power of your identity in Christ magnified.*

It promotes effectiveness as representatives of the greater unseen Kingdom of Heaven to which you belong and which dwells in you. Your ambassadorial role in this world demands that you grow out of careless lifestyles and deeds. The ambassador does not entangle himself/herself in the ways of the citizens of the country of assignment. The Bible says in 2 Timothy 2:4, "No soldier gets entangled in civilian pursuits, since his aim is to please the one who enlisted him."

4. The Seasoning Effect

One seasoning that people use in almost every home is salt. Salt has an innate quality to give a good taste to food. Jesus said in Matthew 5:13, "You are the salt of the earth, but if salt loses its flavor, how shall its saltiness be restored? It is no longer good for anything except to be thrown out and trampled under people's feet." It behooves you to maintain a seasoning effect. You have received this from your identity in Christ so that you can help people around you.

Do not allow your knowledge of scripture puff you up, otherwise, you may cause much friction or bitterness among people instead of seasoning their lives. Understand that wisdom is required to use knowledge you have from the scriptures. Jesus is the wisdom of God and He used His words very carefully to season people's lives. You do not inject yourself in people lives so you would have an issue to use to accuse them.

• Ability to Season

Jesus says in the above passage that you have the innate quality that has a seasoning effect on people to help them in their life situations. This comes from your new identity in Christ. Salt can delay decay to a considerable length depending on the amount applied to meat or other applicable items. One of the qualities of your identity in Christ is this ability to "season". You have the grace to bring flavor to people's troubled lives—the flavor of Christ—so they can also taste His goodness. Because salt makes food taste good to the tongue, it is very common to see people reach for salt when food has no taste.

By His words, Jesus expects you to live as effective seasoning agents in the world. You season people's lives and life situations and issues if you live out who you really are in Christ. Your identity provides the power and anointing to season the bitterness in people's lives spiritually, physically, mentally, or emotionally. You are equipped with the Word of God and the power of the Holy Spirit for this function. Because you practice the qualities of your new self, you affect people's lives and life situations on behalf of Christ.

• Ability to Preserve

Before Jesus left for the cross, He prayed to His God, "While I was with them, I kept them in your name, which you have given me. I have guarded them, and not one of them has been lost except the son of destruction, that the Scripture might be fulfilled" (John 17:12). You have the power of God's

Word and the power of the Holy Spirit. You are able to help people stay off the things that produce decay in their lives so they would focus on Jesus, the true life. You train yourself with the Word of God (Colossians 3:16) so, like Jesus, you would know how to preserve the disciple(s) whom God may bring your way. Jesus said to go make disciples of all nations (Matthew 20:19).

The believer identified with Christ is able to preserve people, not by his/her might or power, but by the Spirit and Word of God. You have to avail yourself for the Holy Spirit's use. You study the Word and learn to hear from the Holy Spirit. The Bible says in 2 Timothy 2:15, "Be diligent to present yourself approved to God, a worker that who does not need to be ashamed, rightly dividing the word of Truth."

Jesus said in John 15:16, "You did not choose Me, but I chose you and appointed you that you should go and bear fruit, and that your fruit should remain, that whatever you ask the Father in My name, He may give you". If you lose your "salt" effect, you lose your ability to help preserve yourself, let alone other people.

Consider wood, metal, plastic, diamond, gold, and water. All of these are affected when they are exposed to salt for a period. In cities where they use salt to melt snow on the streets, the bodies of cars rust faster. As the salt of the earth, you are able to influence the world by the power and authority of your identity in Jesus Christ. In Luke 10:19 Jesus says, "Behold, I give you authority to trample on serpents and scorpions, and over all the power of the enemy, and nothing shall by any means hurt you".

The salt effect within is the anointing of your God-given identity in Jesus. It comes with His authority, power, and dominion to help you reign from the power within your inner self. Apart from Jesus, you can do nothing. If Jesus says you are the salt of the earth, it means His has given you that quality. It is one thing to have the quality of your new identity and another to use it to affect others for their good. The salt influences everything exposed to it, but it retains its saltiness.

If the saltiness in you has quality, your environment cannot influence you. Neither can people's attitudes, or their behaviors. You have the mandate from Jesus to influence your environment and not influenced. Any time your environment influences you, it is an indication that your saltiness lacks quality.

In their transitioning from the Red Sea to the Promised Land, God instructed Moses to erect an altar of incense. He told Moses to make an incense blend, seasoned with salt (Exodus 30:35). Your life, properly oriented as an effective salt of the earth, not only season people's lives, it will also help them present their lives to God as a sweet aroma of incense to the heavenly tabernacle.

As salt of the earth, you do not inject yourself into worldly issues without consultation with your headquarters (Heaven). Incorrectly injecting yourself in worldly issues without such consultation could sometimes backfire and cause you troubles. You do not judge life issues either by worldly views or by the world's media. Jesus said in Mark 9:50b, "Have salt in yourselves, and be at peace with one another". One of the implications in this verse is to fortify yourself against offenses so you can foster peace with people.

5. Participation in the Divine Light

God is light and there is no darkness at all in Him. Darkness is spiritual death. There are no death points (darkness) in God. He is holy. Darkness in people is the fruit produced by the law of sin and death. The law of sin and death produces death points in people who yield to sin and evil ways of the world. It imprisons them in spiritual "tombs". The life of Christ Jesus is the light the world needs to come out of their darkness—their tombs. His light also brings illumination to people so they can come to know God.

The Bible says, "In Him was life, and the life was the light of men" (John 1:4). Jesus said in John 8:12, "I Am the light of the world. Whoever follows me will not walk in darkness, but will have the light of life."

Your identity in Jesus gives you the authority to participate in the divine light of the world with Jesus Christ. The moon reflects the light from the sun; likewise, you reflect the light of Jesus Christ, the Sun of Righteousness. You shine to give light to those bound by darkness (sin) because the light of Christ that you reflect is life. The born-again believer is part of God's light in the world just as Jesus is (Matthew 5:14). Jesus said in John 14:20, "In that day you will know that I am in my Father and you in me, and I in you". What a glorious thought!

God said to Moses, in Leviticus 24:1-2, "Command the people of Israel to bring you pure oil from beaten olives for the lamp, that a light may be kept burning regularly." Your life has gone through many things since you came to Jesus. It is as your life has gone through a "beating" to make you a "pure oil" that will allow the light of God to continually shine through you.

6. Priest and King

Your redemption and the washing you received from Jesus' blood produce a spiritual shift. There is a change in the ownership of your life. An owner of a piece of land will usually place a tag or a sign to let people know who owns the land. God has placed His Spirit in you as a sign of ownership. He who is in you is greater than he who is in the world (1 John 4:4). You have not received the spirit of bondage again to fear, but you have received the Spirit of adoption and you can cry, Abba, Father! (Romans 8:15)

Your priesthood is descended from Jesus, your High Priest. You proclaim the wonderful deeds of your God who took you out of darkness and made you into a unique person. In addition, you become a vessel for God's use, to appeal to people wherever He places you in the world, just as He did through Jesus Christ. As a priest, of the line of Melchisedec, you proclaim God's truths to people. Therefore, equip yourself with knowledge of the truths of God so you will have something to offer to others on God's behalf.

Currently, Jesus is tearing down every rule, thrones, and authority to make way for His kings to rule with Him on His throne. Blessed and holy are you for your part in the first resurrection. The second death would have no power over you. You will become a priest of God and of Christ. You shall reign with Jesus a thousand years (Revelation 20:6). Therefore, you are not only a priest but also a king. Kings carry power and authority. Therefore, Christ is making you a part of a nation of kings to reign with Him on the Earth. How you handle your identity in Christ today will determine your participation in this prestigious position.

Because Christ has made you part of a nation of holy people, it calls for a life of holiness, which God commands you to live. You are in the world but not part of the world's ways and deeds. Consequently, your daily pursuit of the will of God comes along with warfare. This spiritual warfare presses on you on all sides as you press towards your inheritance in Heaven. You go through death to the world and to the flesh. Apostle Paul puts it this way, "For your sake we are killed all day long; We are accounted as sheep for the slaughter" (Romans 8:36). Nevertheless, God always leads you in triumph for your total dependency on Christ.

You can say with Apostle Paul, that in all these things you are more than a conqueror through Jesus. You can say, "…Neither death nor life, nor angels nor principalities nor powers, nor things present nor things to come, nor height nor depth, nor any other created thing, shall be able to separate us from the love of God which is in Christ Jesus our Lord" (Romans 8:38-39).

Chapter 6
Thinking and Speaking Right

The new identity you have in Christ places a demand on you to think and speak correctly and with authority in your life issues. Whether things are going well for you or whether you face challenges and difficulties in life, it is important that you know to speak with the godly nature you have from God. The godly nature does not speak negatively when things happen.

In many ways and in several seasons in life as humans, things happen around us and to us. Whenever these things happen, how you view, perceive, or make of the occurrence is critical, especially as a born-again Christian. I am going to consider why your perception and approach to things that happen in your life is critical. Before I do, I will consider some things to clarify my point.

1. God's Mode of Operation

Everything God does is by and through faith! This is His nature. He calls those things that are not as though they are. Abraham discovered God's nature and mode of operation. Consequently, by faith, he was ready to sacrifice his only son, Isaac, but God stopped him.

God takes delight in people all over the world, who will discover His mode of operation just like Abraham, the father of our faith. Such people believe God with no doubt in their hearts. No matter your life situation, you can believe God. He is not a man that He should lie or change His mind. He waits and watches over His Word (which you must speak) and He will hasten to perform it.

Understand that God created the universe by the power of His spoken Word. Things that you see today came into existence from things that did not exist. By the power of His spoken Word, God called into existence the things in space and in the galaxies. The utterance of God's Word has creative power. The Word was with God; He gave a body to His Word, and He lived among us as Jesus Christ. He was full of God's power and wisdom (John 1:1-5, 14, Hebrews 10:5-7, 1 Corinthians 1:24). Though the universe was not, yet God spoke and it came into existence.

God is a creator and the power of His spoken Word reveals the power of His faith (Hebrews 11:3). He gives life to the dead and calls into existence the things that did not exist (Romans 4:17). There is no creator except God. With God, all things are possible (Mark 10:27). Again the Bible says all things are possible for you if you believe (Mark 9:23). All things are possible for you because you know and understand you have the likeness of God in Christ.

2. Kingdoms Seeking your Attention

Today, the kingdom of the world and the Kingdom of God run side-by-side, but like an inverse proportion. Daily, the Kingdom of God is increasing, while the kingdom of the world is decreasing. A subset of the kingdom of the world is the kingdom of self.

Without our choice, you and I were born into the kingdom of the world. You grew up in it, and taught by its ways. Consequently, you and I defined our life issues by what the world approves and considers as true. The kingdom of the world and the kingdom of self are visible, but the Kingdom of God is unseen. It is spiritual.

Though you see the kingdom of the world as pervading everything in this life, the unseen Kingdom of God is continually eroding its foundation. Daily, men, women, and children accept the redemptive work from Jesus Christ. God transfers them from the kingdom of the world (darkness) into the Kingdom of Jesus Christ (kingdom of light).

3. A Kingdom and Principles

A kingdom has a ruler—a king—and the king have a domain. The king is the god of the kingdom and exercises power and influence over the people who live in his domain. The king has laws or principles that his subjects must live by. The king of the kingdom of self is man. He rules over his own life but is subject to the king of the world.

Satan, though judged, is the god of the kingdom of the world. He makes efforts daily to convince people to define their lives by his principles. He uses blindfolding and fear to advance his cause in this world (2 Corinthians

4:4, Hebrews 2:14-15). The principles of the kingdom of self are self-made principles borrowed from the world. These self-made principles captivate certain people in the "perfect-appearance" attitudes and viewpoints in their life issues, especially in interpersonal relationships. They see others from a lower point of view than themselves.

Jesus said in Mark 14:38 to watch and pray to avoid entering into temptation. One of the greatest temptations you can get yourself into is to allow the world or yourself to define how you live.

Therefore, acknowledge that these kingdoms seek your allegiance. You are the child of God and you have an identity in Christ. Your choice would therefore be to yield to the principle of the Kingdom of God and defy the principles of the world and self. Let the principles of the Kingdom to which you now belong define how you live.

Any opportunities you give to the world or self-will deceive you to live by its principles. Though you are in the world, you do not belong to the world. Even so, you will agree with me that each day, you consciously have to choose to remain out of the world spiritually and mentally, and by your choices and decisions.

LESSON: *The level of your knowledge, understanding, and participation in your new identity in Christ will define the level of influence the world can have on your life. The world's influence will show up in your thoughts, declarations, or speech.*

When a Christian has difficulty denying the influence of the principles of the world, it shows a lack of practice of the attributes of their new identity in Christ Jesus. Because you have an identity in Christ, God wants you to live and function through Jesus, His son (1 John 4:9). If you want to experience a mighty move of God in and through your life, the principles of the Kingdom of God have to help you die to the world and to the kingdom of self.

To help you live or define your life issues by the principles of His Kingdom, God has given you His precious and very great promises to live by (2 Peter 1:3-4). He also has given you all spiritual blessings in the heavenly places (Ephesians 1:3). Because God has recreated you in His likeness, learn not to apply to your life, everything the world defines as true. Jesus is your role model and "Consultant". He lived in this world but functioned by the principles of the Kingdom of God. He did not define His life issues by what the world approves as true and acceptable.

4. Living by Kingdom Principles

Writing about Jesus, the prophet Isaiah said, "His delight shall be in the fear of the Lord. He shall not judge by what His eyes see, or decide disputes by what His ears hear" (Isaiah 11:3). I pronounce this spirit to come upon you. You will learn not to judge by what your eyes see or by what your ears hear. Jesus said to Pilate, "My kingdom is not of this world. If my kingdom were of this world, my servants would have been fighting, that I might not be delivered over to the Jews. But my kingdom is not from the world" (John 18:36).

You have God's likeness in your new identity in Christ. Therefore, God expects your thought processes and declarations to help you live and function by the principles of the Kingdom of God just as Jesus did. It is warfare to live entirely by the principles of the Kingdom of God. Therefore, pray daily for more grace to deepen your stand in Jesus in whom you abide. The principle of the Kingdom of God is the power of faith and love, expressed through righteousness, godliness, and holiness all through obedience.

In Exodus 14:13-16, Moses said to the children of Israel, "Fear not, stand firm, and see the salvation of the Lord, which He will work for you today. For the Egyptians whom you see today, you shall never see again." This sounds like an excellent way to encourage a people trapped between the Red Sea and the army of their former masters.

Nevertheless, God heard and saw the situation differently. God saw Moses, a leader with power in his staff and yet crying to Him. The Lord said to Moses, "Why do you cry to me? Tell the people of Israel to go forward. Lift up your staff, and stretch out your hand over the sea and divide it, that the people of Israel may go through the sea on dry ground" (Exodus 14:13-16). That was very interesting! God expected Moses to use the power He had invested in his staff to divide the Red Sea.

Today, God has invested His exceeding great power to work on your behalf (Ephesians 1:19-20). This is the same power God exerted to raise Christ from the dead, and seated Him at His right hand of authority in the heavenly places. Learn to use this power of God that works for you. Declare and divide the many seemingly "Red Seas" that come in your life. Speak God's promises in your challenging times and He will hasten to perform what you say.

Moses, Joshua, Elijah, and many other people of God in the Old Covenant spoke and declared creative words to change their life situations or environments. In Christ Jesus, you are a man or woman of God because of your baptism with His Spirit.

5. Jesus' Faith Declaration

When Jesus came on the "world scene", His power to speak creatively became one that the world had never seen. Jesus walked the earth in our form. He functioned by faith, by the principles of the Kingdom to which He belongs! By faith, He turned water into the best wine at a wedding ceremony. By faith, He spoke to a fig tree and it withered to the root. By faith, He commanded the raging sea to still. By faith, He made the dead live again. By faith, He made the blind to see again and the lame and cripple to walk again.

In Mark 4:35, Jesus said to the disciples, "Let us go across to the other side." This means they had to cross the sea to get to the other side. While in the sea, a great windstorm arose and the waves were breaking into the boat so that the boat was already filling with water. Terrified, the disciples woke up Jesus, who then rebuked the wind, saying, "Peace! Be still!" (Mark 4:39). The wind ceased, and there was a great calm.

The point of my interest is from the question Jesus asked the disciples in Mark 4:40, "Why are you so afraid? Have you still no faith?" Jesus' question indicates that He was expecting the disciples to have had enough faith to do what they had seen Him do many times, irrespective of the difference in the current situation. He was expecting them to command the wind to cease.

I will consider two other situations of interest:

1) As Jesus came from the mount of transfiguration, the father of an epileptic child told Him that His disciples were not able to heal his child. Hearing the man, Jesus answered, "O faithless and twisted generation, how long am I to be with you? How long am I to bear with you? Bring him here to me" (Matthew 17:14-17). Here again, Jesus expected the disciples to have had the faith to heal the epileptic child.

2) Jesus and His disciples were returning from Bethany one morning. He was hungry and, seeing a fig tree, went to seek figs. The fig tree had no figs, only leaves. Jesus said to the fig tree, "May no fruit ever come from you again!" The fig tree withered at once. When the disciples saw it, they marveled, saying, "How did the fig tree wither at once?" Jesus answered them, "Have faith in God. Truly, I say to you, whoever says to this mountain, 'Be taken up and thrown into the sea,' and does not doubt in his heart, but believes that what he says will come to pass, it will be done for him" (Mark 11:12-23).

Never belittle yourself! God has invested dynamic power in your inner self as a born-again believer baptized with the Holy Spirit. God is "processing" you to become a man or woman who will speak life and creative words as a ruler in Christ's Kingdom. Jesus is your example of what God wants to do through you. Speak creatively into your life situations and into other people's lives. Your conformation is into the image of Jesus Christ, the One by whom the entire universe came into being. He declares and it happens!

Learn to speak to your life situations with the power of the godly nature you have received as a born-again believer in Christ. In your life situations, speak to yourself based on your knowledge of God's Word and His faithfulness. Today, Jesus is saying to you, "If you have faith and do not doubt, you will not only do what has been done to the fig tree, but even if you say to this mountain, 'Be taken up and thrown into the sea,' it will happen" (Matthew 21:21).

Authority to Speak Creatively—Getting to the Point

When things happen in your life, you can perceive them in many ways. Your perception will define what comes out of your mouth. When things happen in your life, what do you see and what do you say? As I indicated earlier, you have the godly nature as one of the attributes of your new identity in Christ. Therefore, you have the authority to speak creatively from a faith-motivated perception. You have to speak from what your "eye of faith" sees and not from what your natural eyes see.

Why is Jesus expecting you and me to think and speak creatively with authority? The basis of His expectation is who you have become in Him. As I referred to earlier, God has recreated you and me anew in the power of His likeness, in righteousness with true holiness. With God's likeness in you, He wants you to deny the ways the world thinks and speaks. Satan motivates the way the world thinks and speaks. They (of the world) do so according to his principles. You are in the world but not of it.

The seventy-two disciples whom Jesus sent out returned from their evangelistic mission, rejoicing that the demons were subject to them in the name of Jesus. Jesus said in Luke 10:19, "Behold, I have given you authority to tread on serpents and scorpions, and over all the power of the enemy, and nothing shall hurt you". Therefore, in addition to God's likeness, you have Jesus' authority to overcome spiritual powers of evil, and over all the power of the enemy.

What you declare and what the body of Christ declares will happen, and nothing that the enemies of God do can hinder you. What you declare must be righteous and conform to God's promise for you. What happened on the mission of the seventy-two was a foretaste of the Christian life that believers were to live out in their daily lives.

Jesus said in Acts 1:8, "But you will receive power when the Holy Spirit has come upon you, and you will be My witnesses in Jerusalem and in all Judea and Samaria, and to the end of the earth." Because you have a new identity in Christ and the baptism of the Holy Spirit, the power of God is ready to work through your daily life and through your declarations. God waits on you to think and speak correctly with authority.

Jesus, asked the disciples, "But who do you say that I am?" Simon Peter replied, "You are the Christ, the Son of the living God." Jesus answered him, "Blessed are you, Simon Bar-Jonah, for flesh and blood has not revealed this to you, but My Father who is in heaven. I tell you, you are Peter, and on this rock I will build my church, and the gates of hell shall not prevail against it. I will give you the keys of the kingdom of heaven, and whatever you bind on earth shall be bound in heaven, and whatever you loose on earth shall be loosed in heaven" (Matthew 16:15-19).

Jesus is building His church with people who know Him as Christ, Son of the living God. This is not an intellectual knowledge. It is revelation knowledge that will influence you to submit to Jesus through obedience and trust. Because you learn to submit to Christ through obedience and trust, it brings you to conversion. He blesses you with the keys of the Kingdom of Heaven to bind and loose on the earth.

Today, Jesus has given to His church the ability to speak creatively. What the church says, the powers of hell will not have the power to resist or prevail against it. Like Jesus, in relation to His Father, the church-which includes you-has to learn to say and do what Jesus is saying. The words of Jesus carry power and authority because His words are from His Father. If you declare what Jesus says, even the promises of God, it will transform your life situations, and will accomplish God's will in your life.

Jesus says to you in Matthew 18:18, "Truly, I say to you, whatever you bind on earth shall be bound in heaven, and whatever you loose on earth shall be loosed in heaven." Therefore, take heed to how you think and what you say in your life situations. Avoid careless and unfruitful thinking or declarations. Let the Word of God and His promises define your thought processes and declarations. Do not let your life challenges or problems cause you to think and speak carelessly.

Learn to speak the promises that God has promised you. God will endorse His promises in heaven as you declare them in the earth. When you fail to declare God's promises into your situation, you deny the opportunity to demonstrate the power of your new identity in Christ. You also deny God the glory due Him. You and I, and all believers, constitute the church or the body of Christ. Therefore, you have the authority to speak creatively just like the men of God of old. Jesus says you can do greater things because He is now at the right hand of God's authority and power. He wants to flow through you in your daily life issues.

God is in the process of conforming you into the image of His son, Jesus Christ. Therefore, learn to use the promises of God to declare words of faith in your life situations. It will help you to escape corruption. That way, you can become powerful in your declarations. This is so because God has called you to escape corruption so you will participate in His divine nature. He has given you authority to declare those things (that no eyes have seen) as though they are.

God has placed you with Christ in Himself and your faith grows and gains divine power in Christ. He expects you to walk not by what your natural eyes see, but by the eyes of your faith (2 Corinthians 5:7). God wants to show His manifold wisdom through you. It will show His handiwork for taking you, who was nothing, but is now transforming you into the image of His son. It will show how He has filled you with His Holy Spirit. God wants to display, before the rulers and authorities in the heavenly places (Ephesians 3:10), what He has accomplished in you through Christ.

God wants you to think and talk right like Him. He wants you to think and see success when others see failure. He wants you to think and see breakthrough when others see a dead-end. He wants you to think and see cancer healed and removed from your body when the doctors see otherwise.

God wants you not to view His promises as mere words on the pages of the Bible. He wants you to see the Bible as your power manual, applicable in every situation in your life. When things happen in your life, God wants you to use the godly nature of your new identity in Christ to think correctly and therefore, speak authoritatively and creatively. Do not allow your thinking and your declarations to put you down!

When things happen in your life, test it before you speak. Test if there is anything that conforms to the principles of God's Kingdom to which you belong. If you find anything that lines up with God's Kingdom principles, irrespective of significance, learn to focus on that and begin to speak creatively. Refuse to speak about the grim side of the issues of life. Speaking on the grim side of life issues enhances the work of the kingdom of the world (darkness). The world dwells on the negative, on the dismal, and it is going down because God has judged the ruler of the world, Satan.

As I pointed out earlier, God has assigned angels to help His people. They wait on you to speak words they can use to work for you. Refuse to speak or declare the grim side of what the natural eyes can see when things happen in your life. If you speak creatively and positively, angels will hasten to perform your declaration of God's Word. Why is that? Because what you speak creatively and positively come from the Word and promises of God.

It was true that the daughter of Jairus died because the needs of other people delayed Jesus on His way to Jairus' house. It is a fact that if a person is dead, there are signs that prove death has occurred! Notwithstanding, when Jesus reached Jairus' house, He said the child was not dead but sleeping. Jesus spoke according to His faith convictions based on the principles of the Kingdom He belong. Jesus spoke and the child rose from the dead. This brought glory and honor to God!

In one of his evangelistic journeys, Apostle Paul stopped at Troas. On the first day of the week, he met with the believers to break bread. Paul addressed the people until midnight. During these hours, a young man named Eutychus drifted off into a deep sleep. Sitting at the window, he fell down from the third story and they picked him up as dead. Apostle Paul went down, bent over him, took him into his arms, and said, "Stop being alarmed, because he is still alive". They picked up the young man alive and were greatly relieved" (Act 20:6-12).

The Bible says the believer lives by faith and not by sight. It is a choice you have to make! You have the liberty to choose what you want to think or declare out of your mouth in your life issues. Though you have this liberty, yet, if you think and speak negatively, it will not help you because it will not accomplish what you want (1 Corinthians 10:23).

Note that whatever name Adam assigned to the creatures that God brought to him, that became their name. You have to learn to speak or "prophesy" into your own life, irrespective of what you see with your natural eyes. "What no eye has seen, nor ear heard, nor the heart of man imagined, what God has prepared for those who love Him" (1Corinthians 2:9). Those who love God use His Word to define their life issues (1John 5:3) and they obey God's Word.

If you have trained yourself to perceive from the negative point of view, now you know the power that accompanies your new identity in Christ. You have to start speaking with the godly nature you have received and the angels of God will hasten to perform your righteous words.

Without your choice, you were born into this world and trained by it. Your thought processes and approach to life were subject to the principles of the kingdom of the world until you met Christ. The fallen human thinking usually tilts to the negative when things happen. It tilts towards the worst! The worldly nature easily speaks negatively when things happen.

God is in the process of making your final nature into the image of Jesus Christ. Today, He commands you to practice your godly nature. Learn to think and speak creatively or positively according to the principles of God's Kingdom. One of the reasons God wants you to renew your mind is to know His will to help you live by the principles of His Kingdom. This is how you can see miracles happen for you in this world.

You are a unique person, recreated in Christ to carry the fullness of God (Ephesians 3:19). Nevertheless, you have to choose to yield to the demands your new creation places on you.

You see, Elijah made a declaration and for three years, there was no rain in the land. Then he declared in prayer that it should rain, but nothing happened. For six times his servant reported to him that there was no cloud to indicate imminent rain. On the seventh time, the servant saw a cloud like the size of a man's hand. Elijah declared it was going to rain and it did! You see, Elijah did not wait for a vast amount of clouds in the sky to prove to him it would rain. The size of cloud the servant saw, though insignificant, was enough for Elijah to declare it was going to rain, and it did (1Kings 18:41-45).

Like Elijah, when things happen, learn to look for something, irrespective of size or significance, that is true, of good report, worthy of praise, commendable, and lovely. Then, do as Elijah did—use that to declare faith-motivated things according to the will of God for you. Refuse to declare the things you do not want to happen in your life. How long do you have to declare the positive? You declare until it happens. Elijah prayed seven times before he saw an insignificant-sized cloud in the sky. You have to declare what will honor and bring praise to God. If it will not bring honor to the God you serve, refuse to let it come out of your mouth.

In the book of Joshua, God delivered the Amorites into the hands of the children of Israel. Joshua and his army were in the process of conquering the enemy. Unfortunately, the sun was going down and Joshua needed more time to finish with the job of getting rid of the enemy. Joshua stood before Israel and commanded the sun to stand still over Gibeon and the moon to stand in its place in the Aijalon Valley. The sun and the moon did as Joshua commanded. At Joshua's command, not only did the sun stand still, but the moon as well, until they conquered the enemies (Joshua 10:12-14).

There is corruption all around you in this world but Jesus has given you authority to declare God's Word with authority, in order to make things happen for you and for others. Therefore, orient your mind and heart to acknowledge the power and authority inherent in your identity in Christ.

Cease declaring self-defeating words or indulging in negative views of what happens in your life or around you. Use Christ's authority to declare what the angels assigned to you can use to help you. See what God has prepared for you with your eye of faith and declare to the hearing of your God. Your God will hasten to perform His Word, which you declare, to glorify His own name. The world will know that you are a unique individual and have Christ with you.

Because your new self has the God nature, He expects you to speak like your Father in Heaven. When things happen in your life, take heed to what your mind thinks, because. if not checked, it will become the words you speak. Your heart will pick up what your mouth says about your situation. Out of the abundance of the heart, your mouth will continue to speak. What you speak carries power! Proverbs 18:20-21 says, "From the fruit of a man's mouth his stomach is satisfied; he is satisfied by the yield of his lips. Death and life are in the power of the tongue, and those who love it will eat its fruits."

If death and life are in the power of a man's tongue, how much greater will this power be for a man redeemed, sanctified, and filled with the Holy Spirit? Will he not function like Jesus? Life situations and environments will bow to God's Word as you declare it with your faith.

When situations get out of line with the will of God for you or for your family, confront it with the Word of His promises. The Word of God cannot fail. God compares His Word with the rain and the snow. These do not return to Heaven when they come down from Heaven. Likewise, God says in Isaiah 55:11 "So shall my word be that goes out from my mouth. It shall not return to me empty, but it shall accomplish that which I purpose, and shall succeed in the thing for which I sent it."

Therefore, you can trust that as you declare the Word of God, it will accomplish His purpose in your life situation or environment. The Word, or promises, of God has gone through vigorous testing and been tried over the ages, yet has always proven to be powerful, true, and pure (Psalm 12:6; Psalm 18:30). It possesses creative power and it is ready to help you if you will handle it with a strong conviction of faith. It is very important that you declare God's Word in your times of need with the conviction of faith. Your conviction of faith pulls the things you say from the unseen into the seen to the glory of God.

As a candidate of salvation, there are angels assigned to serve and help you (Hebrews 1:13-14). They wait on your words that line up with God's promises so they will work for you. If you find it difficult to stand alone in your faith declarations, get another spirit-filled believer to accompany you in this journey of faith declaration. Jesus said in Matthew 18:19-20, "Again I say to you, if two of you agree on earth about anything they ask, it will be done for them by my Father in Heaven. For where two or three are gathered in my name, there am I among them."

Therefore, remember! Do not dwell on the negative or adverse aspects of what is going on in your life or is happening in your environment. Avoid becoming a victim mentally to statements by people such as the following, "This disease runs in my family, and I fear I am going to be a victim". Judge if this is the correct faith statement a believer filled with the Holy Spirit should make.

How could a Christian think and make such a statement when God says in Philippians 4:8 to think on what is true and praiseworthy? The truth is God's promise to you, "No weapon that is formed against you shall be blessed; and every tongue that shall rise against you in judgment, you shall condemn (Isaiah 54:17). God says this promise is your inheritance because you serve Him. In addition, you have an identity in Jesus Christ."

What are true in your life are God's promises, or His Word. If what is happening does not line up with the Word of God or His promise for you, then it is false. Do not allow what has happened to your siblings or parents cause you to make such statement as the above. In addition, do not let it take your heart down the path to anxiety. As a born again, spirit-filled child of God, refuse to let negative statements against you (or the thing happening in your life), define who you are.

If you do not know what to say in response to what people say about you, be still until the Holy Spirit gives you what to say! Do not invite the "Job factor" into your life. Before his calamities happened, Job allowed his thoughts to dwell on negative expectations. Job said, "For the thing that I fear comes upon me, and what I dread befalls me" (Job 3:25).

Grow your faith in God's Word today before your day of need comes. Then, when your need comes, you will have clearness of heart and boldness to look for something you can dwell on, and to declare powerful words into your situation. Do not wait to see or feel something significant before you declare the promises of God in your situation. Let your eye of faith see your victory and have courage and boldness to speak faith declarations in your situation until you see your victory.

Command your situation to come into alignment with God's Word or promise to you. Remember, Elijah sent out his servant six times to look for cloud but it was not until the seventh time, that he saw a cloud like the hand of a man. That was very insignificant size of cloud but Elijah focused on what was insignificant and began to declare it was going to rain and soon, the heavens grew dark with cloud and heavy rain fell that day (1Kings 18:44-45).

Therefore, when things happen in your life or in your environment, perceive, and measure them against God's Word. Find something in the confusion or out of the chaos that line up with God's promise. Then, focus on that thing and use it to declare a creative word into your situation or environment. Understand that Elijah did not wait for the entire sky to darken with clouds before he declared imminent rain. He focused on the tiny cloud that the servant saw to declare that it was going to rain and it did. Failure to think correctly about your life situations will activate negative confessions of what is happening.

Learn to use the godly nature of your new identity in Christ to speak creatively like your Father in Heaven. Do not wait until everyone agrees with what you think about God's promises before you declare your conviction of faith. You work with God and you do not need anyone's permission to declare "good" when it looks "dire". Declare it is good when everyone says it is dire! God will hasten to perform what you say.

God Responds to His Word

In Jeremiah 1:11-12, God said to the prophet, "What do you see? The prophet said, "I see a rod of an almond tree." Again, God said to Jeremiah, "You have seen well; for I will watch over My Word to perform it". God is asking you and I the same question today. When things happen in your life, how do you perceive them? How you perceive and what you speak are very critical. Therefore, if you do not know what to say, take heed to what the eyes of your heart sees and what your mind thinks. In addition, it is important to note that as a man thinks in his heart, so is he (Proverbs 23:7). Out of the abundance of the heart, the mouth will speak (Luke 6:45).

If you truly believe in the promises God has given you in Christ, how you think and speak in your time of trouble will prove it. You have to believe the mighty hand of God is ready to take over what deviates from His will for you and to give you the victory in your situation. Therefore, learn to speak correctly by declaring God's promises in every one of your situations.

LESSON: *If you claim to believe God's promises, how you think and what you say out of your mouth when things happen will prove where you are in your belief.*

LESSON: *Do not define God's power by the magnitude of your life's problems or challenges. Rather, learn to define your situations, problems, and challenges by the overwhelming power of God. Everything in the universe will bow to Jesus, who is God's Word.*

Joshua spoke to the sun and it stood still. Jesus spoke to the fig tree and it withered to the root. He spoke to the raging sea and it quieted. Jesus says to you, "Let not your heart be troubled. Believe in God; believe also in me" (John 14:1). If you believe, learn to speak to your situations and see them bow to the Word of God, Jesus Christ.

Your new identity in Christ comes with tremendous power. Therefore, know who you have become in Christ. Whenever things happen in your life, mount up courage and boldly declare the promises of God over your situation and see the angels work for you.

Chapter 7
Yielding to God's Purposes

The Christian life is a call to a purposeful lifestyle. It is a lifestyle motivated by the principles of the Kingdom of God. The desire to live by the principles of the Kingdom of God will draw your focus and desire to walk in the attributes of your identity in Christ Jesus.

In the pursuit of God's purposes for your life, you may sometimes come into seasons where you will feel like He has abandoned you. You may not be able to experience His presence the way you used to. Despite that feeling, God is nearer to you than you think. He draws you to a place of purpose, and a place where you will understand Him better. Your understanding of God enhances your ability to trust Him even in your very difficult times and seasons. Again, your trust in God and dependency on the Holy Spirit enhances a purposeful Christian life, which is a Holy Spirit-led life.

God's desire is that your life will be in accord with His Spirit. He wants you to come to the place in your life where the Spirit of God is the one who leads you just as He led Jesus. As you learn to escape corruption in the world, you participate in the divine nature of God. You will come to understand the importance of living and walking by the Spirit of God. The vision of the prophet Ezekiel in Chapter 1 shows an illustration of a Spirit-led life.

Orient your life to the knowledge and understanding of your new identity in Christ and the demand it places on your daily life. You are in the Son of God and therefore, He wants you to learn to work out His purposes for your life. Success in the pursuit of His purposes for your life enhances because you learn to live and walk by His Spirit. Ezekiel Chapter 1 says that wherever the Spirit went, the living creatures went, and the wheels went beside them.

Power to Fulfill Christ's Commission

Before Jesus left to go to His Father, He commanded His followers to go into the entire world and proclaim the Gospel to the whole creation. He who believes and is baptized shall be saved, but he who does not believe will be condemned (Mark 16:15-16). Belief comes with repentance. God has chosen you as part of a special race. He has received you as His own possession. He has made you a part of His royal priesthood and a holy nation. His goal is that you will proclaim His Excellencies, how He has brought you into His marvelous light and given you a new identity in Christ (1 Peter 2:9).

As I indicated earlier, your identity comes with power—the resurrection power in your innermost being. It works mightily because you orient your life to its demands—godliness, righteousness, and holiness. In addition, Jesus said you receive power when the Holy Spirit comes upon you. You receive this power to become a witness to Him in all places. As a Christian, you are to live as an "evangelist".

- You are a reconciliation agent for Christ—2 Corinthians 5:18-19.
- You are an ambassador for Christ. He wants to make His appeal to people through you—2 Corinthians 5:20.
- You reach all people across gender, race, and ethnic lines.
- Christ assigns His people to reach people in different sectors of the world, e.g., Apostle Peter to the Jews and Apostle Paul to the Gentiles.

The power of Christ that you receive gives you an effective ministry to people beginning with your own home. The power of your identity is the power Christ has assigned to help you live a purposeful Christian life. It will help you use the Gospel to do the following (among many):

- Maintain a godly home
- Follows Christ's example
- Lead others by serving:

  o In your family and in the church—no bossy attitude
  o With humility
  o To honor Christ with obedience

Purposeful Living

The Bible says in Hosea 4:6a, "My people are destroyed for lack of knowledge". To lack the knowledge of God is to lack the knowledge of one's purpose.

LESSON: *True accomplishment is to discover and fulfill God's assignment for your life without corrupting yourself. When knowledge of your purpose is lacking, this presents the likelihood of misusing life opportunities and corrupting self in life experiences.*

Jesus knew His purpose at a young age. After spending time in Jerusalem at the feast of the Passover, as the family returned back to Nazareth, Jesus stayed behind. The parents realized Jesus was not with them. Therefore, they returned to Jerusalem to seek Him. Fortunately, they found Him in the temple with the teachers. (Luke 2:41-46) How proud a parent would be to have a child who loves the things of God?

His parents said to Him, "Son, why have you treated us so? Behold, your father and I have been searching for you in a great distress." Jesus answered them, "Why were you looking for Me? Did you not know that I must be about My Father's business?" (Luke 2:48-49). The parents did not understand the word Jesus spoke to them. The words of this young boy were "big" talk—a young boy who knew His purpose? That was very interesting and unheard of.

When David became king over Israel, he concluded that the Lord had established him as king and exalted his kingdom in order to benefit His people Israel (2 Samuel 5:12). So King David knew why God made him king. Like King David, I pray that all national leaders, even religious leaders, will discover why God has placed them in leadership.

LESSON: *The level of success is defined not just by the level of financial or material accomplishments but it is more so by the level of purpose completed.*

Jesus told a crowd of people in Capernaum, "I have come down from Heaven, not to do My own will but the will of Him who sent Me. And this is the will of Him who sent Me, that I should lose nothing of all that He has given Me, but raise it up on the last day" (John 6:38-39).

Because Jesus knew His purpose on the earth, He knew when He had accomplished that purpose. He prayed to the Father, "I have glorified You on the earth. I have finished the work which You have given Me to do" (John 17:4).

LESSON: *Where purpose is known, there is a high possibility of realizing when it is accomplished. In addition, it is possible to know when deviation has occurred.*

Much of the chaos, rebellion, self-will, and evil in this world is the result of the people's lack of knowledge of God's purpose for placing them where they are. When people in places of authority and political power misuse or abuse their power, it is a sure sign that they lack knowledge of God's purpose for placing them where they are.

Heaven is disappointed when some Christian leaders misuse their position to amass wealth beyond spiritual common sense. Jesus said the abundance of possessions does not define the accomplishment of one's life. Therefore, He said in Luke 12:15, "Take care, and beware of covetousness, for one's life does not consist in the abundance of the things he possesses".

The servant of Elisha, Gehazi, failed to become the next Elisha because he lost focus of his purpose as a servant of the man of God. He did not learn from his master, Elisha. Greed and love for money distracted him. His master, Elisha, received double anointing from Elijah because he was purpose driven. He did not lose his purpose even though Elijah tried several times to get him to turn aside from following him. Elisha did not allow anything to distract him from his purpose—to receive a double anointing from his master, Elijah.

In his captivity in Babylon, Daniel knew his God and his purpose. Therefore, he resolved that he would not defile himself with the king's food or with the wine that he drank. He asked the chief of the eunuchs to allow him not to defile himself (Daniel 1:8).

LESSON: *The lack of purpose in life produces a wasteful lifestyle: mentally, spiritually, or financially. Pursuit of purpose is not what you do but what God has created you to do.*

LESSON: *Guard against purpose, driven by love for money. When love for money drives you into a presumed purpose, you could likely pursue enriching yourself by the wealth around you, irrespective of who it belongs. When you are living your purpose, you delight in what you do more than any inner drive to enrich yourself with what you do. You see what you do as opportunity to exhibit excellence for people to see God's glory.*

God's Purpose for the Christian

Part of the purpose of God for the Christian is the formation of the full stature of Christ in the inner self. Therefore, He wants you to learn to conform to His will through a life of obedience. He wants you to offer your body to Him as a living sacrifice. Upon a total offering of your life, God will fashion and use you to help other people in their difficult life issues, which will help them overcome just as you have. Apostle Paul said to Timothy, "And the things that thou hast heard of me among many witnesses, the same commit thou to faithful men, who shall be able to teach others also" (2 Timothy 2:2 KJV).

God is bringing the world into conformity to His word, from which humanity deviated. The Bible says in Hebrews 5:8-10 (KJV), "Though He were a Son, yet learned He obedience by the things which He suffered; And being made perfect, He became the author of eternal salvation unto all them that obey Him; Called of God an high priest after the order of Melchisedec."

Your salvation does not only provide the possibility of entering Heaven, but places a demand on you to learn obedience to God. Your life of obedience makes you a candidate to receive the transformation processes into the image of Jesus, who obeyed God completely.

Ruth, the Woman of Purpose

Naomi was the mother-in-law to Ruth in the land of Moab. The husband of Naomi was Elimelech, who had passed away, along with their sons. Ruth, a Moabite woman who had married one of Naomi's sons, was determined to return to Bethlehem with Naomi. Naomi said, "See, your sister-in-law has gone back to her people and to her gods; return after your sister-in-law".

Ruth answered Naomi, "Do not urge me to leave you or to return from following you. For where you go I will go and where you lodge I will lodge. Your people shall be my people and your God my God. Where you die I will die, and there will I be buried. May the LORD do so to me and more also if anything but death part me from you." And when Naomi saw that she was determined to go with her, she said no more" (Ruth 1:15-18).

Acknowledge the Law of the Spirit of Life

"There is therefore now no condemnation to those who are in Christ Jesus, who do not walk according to the flesh, but according to the Spirit. For the law of the Spirit of life in Christ Jesus has made me free from the law of sin and death" (Romans 8:1-2).

To talk about the law of the Spirit of life in Christ Jesus, you must understand another law—the law of sin and death. The law of sin and death is a constraining force that hinders the majority of humanity from conforming to the will of God in their life issues. It prevents them from living to God's pleasure. It draws many people into fleshly and worldly lifestyles, far below God's expectation or desire. This law has ability to introduce darkness and ultimately death in your life is you let it. It is the law of sin that controls the fallen nature. God wants His fullness in you so learn to walk in love for God and for people (Ephesians 3:16-19).

You are in Christ; therefore, you overcome the law of sin and death because you live by the Spirit of God in you. The greater law in Christ Jesus, which is the "law of the Spirit of life", gives you the power to do so. Because you abide in Jesus and have an identity in Him, the greater law in Him sets you free from the constraining force of the law of sin and death.

I do not know your country of citizenship, but in the United States of America, there is a high court in each state. In addition, there is a federal court called the Supreme Court. If a citizen is dissatisfied with the ruling in a state's high court and appeals to the Supreme Court, the rulings of the Supreme Court reverses or upholds the ruling of the state court. The power of the law of the Spirit of life in Christ Jesus overrules the effects of the law of sin and death for all who abide in Jesus and live by the Spirit of God. This is how you can escape condemnation.

The "Supreme Court" of Heaven arbitrates your case and it gives you victory over any other law that could otherwise imprison you in a life below your status in Christ. Therefore, the Bible says in Colossians 2:6-7, "As you received Christ Jesus the Lord, so walk in Him, rooted, and built up in Him and established in the faith, just as you were taught, abounding in thanksgiving".

The law of sin and death can teach you to hold an unending grudge against those who offend you. The law of the Spirit of life in Christ will teach you to forgive those who offend you. It teaches you to practice Romans 12:18-21, "If it is possible, as much as it depends on you, live peaceably with all men. Beloved, do not avenge yourselves, but rather give place to wrath; for it is written, "Vengeance is Mine, I will repay," says the Lord." Therefore, "If your enemy is hungry, feed him; if he is thirsty, give him a drink; For in so doing you will heap coals of fire on his head". Do not be overcome by evil, but overcome evil with good."

The only power that sets people free from the law of sin and death is the law of the Spirit of life in Christ Jesus. This law is Light and Life and it revives or gives freedom to those who are in Christ and who live by the Spirit. Because you are born-again, the law of the Spirit of life is the law that increasingly rules and directs your life. It is the law of the new covenant, which guides you when you decide to live a Spirit-led life.

Anyone who subscribes to this law of the Spirit of life will produce fruit, the fruit of the Spirit. You have to realize that in the Christian life, you do not just lay back and presume the Lord will do everything for you. He needs your cooperation. It is always "the sword of the Lord and of Gideon" (Judges 7:20 KJV). It is also the mighty hand of God and Jehoshaphat's trust and praises (2Chronicles 20:22-24).

Galatians 5:22-26 (KJV) says, "But the fruit of the Spirit is love, joy, peace, longsuffering, gentleness, goodness, faith, meekness, temperance: against such there is no law. And they that are Christ's have crucified the flesh with the affections and lusts. If we live in the Spirit, let us also walk in the Spirit. Let us not be desirous of vain glory, provoking one another, envying one another."

Those who belong to Christ Jesus receive the power of the law of the Spirit of life to crucify the flesh with its passions and desires. If you live by the Spirit, learn also to walk by the Spirit. The conceited life, provoking one another, envying one another, and the like are no longer a part of your new life in Christ. These are not the attitudes and lifestyles of the higher life in Christ Jesus.

The law of the Spirit of the life in Christ Jesus leads you in the ways of godliness, righteousness, and holiness. It conditions you and provides the ability to think right, talk right, and to act right, especially in your interpersonal relationships. Lack of the fruit of the Spirit in your life is an indication your roots are not correctly sucking from the life in Jesus. Examine the grounds on which you are building your faith and trust. When correctly built up, and established in Christ, your faith and trust in Christ grows and the law of the Spirit of life in Christ leads you in a lifestyle that escapes condemnation. Learn to "bolt" your life to the solid foundation in Jesus for a consistent Holy Spirit-led life.

To live by the Spirit, learn obedience to God's Word and the voice of the Holy Spirit in both the significant and insignificant things in your life. Learn to avoid overruling the Word of God and the voice of the Holy Spirit for your self-will. Then, learn to obey God in the significant issues of your life. Avoid executing evil thoughts and imaginations that the devil suggests to your mind. Avoid planning evil against your fellow man.

Use your new godly nature in Christ to pray covenant prayers against anything that could lead you to practice evil. That is one of the ways to walk in the fear of the Lord. You have the godly nature and therefore, avoid any imprisonment from the law of sin and death. You can find a record of some the effects of the law of sin and death in Galatians 5:19-21.

God has made you a royal priest and a king in Christ Jesus. You are an ambassador for Christ. You are a part of a holy nation. Yield to God and daily pray the following prayer: *"Father, I stand in the authority you have given me in Christ Jesus. I bring under subjection to Jesus Christ anything in my life that could contend against my ability to enlarge in You and You in me. I pray that Jesus' blood will remove and destroy these things from my life, in Jesus' name."*

God Provides Help

In addition to His grace and precious promises, God gets His feet wet with your daily life issues and His call to you to work out your salvation. His desire is that what you do daily as a Christian will please Him. The Bible calls on you to do God's will. Doing God's will is how you please Him and it gets you into Heaven. Jesus said in Matthew 7:21-23, "Not everyone who says to Me, 'Lord, Lord,' shall enter the kingdom of heaven, but he who does the will of My Father in heaven, Many will say to Me in that day, Lord, Lord, have we not prophesied in Your name, cast out demons in Your name, and done many wonders in Your name? And then I will declare to them, I never knew you; depart from Me, you who practice lawlessness."

The Father wants to change your inner nature into that of Jesus Christ's, who did His will perfectly. For that reason, He provides you with the help that you need. The Bible says in Philippians 2:13, "For it is God who works in you both to will and to do for His good pleasure." I will therefore consider what I refer to as the transistor/receiver phenomenon.

• The Transmitter/Receiver Phenomenon

As I indicated earlier, God wants His people, washed by the blood of His son, to live purposeful lives in this world. Therefore, He works in you to help you do His will, which is what pleases Him.

Most of you may have a radio in your home or on your cell phone. The radio speaks and plays music, but if you open it up you will not find an actual person inside. The radio functions as a receiver, which receives transmissions from radio stations. The radio speaks or plays music exactly as was transmitted from the stations. God says He will work in you to help you do what pleases Him. Therefore, He wants you to receive His work in you—what He transmits— so that, like the radio, you will do exactly what He works in you.

Christians differ in their responses to God's work in their lives because they differ in the level of their Christian experiences and focus. Consequently, they differ in their effectiveness as "receivers" of God's "transmissions" or motivations. Determine to be an effective receiver to receive God's transmissions and follow through in obedience.

Any problem inside of the receiver will offset its function. It will not give out correct information to the hearers. Oftentimes, other waves interfere with the ability of the receiver to give accurate sounds. Unlike natural transmitters, God transmits continually and clearly and His voice is accurate and exact. Any interference will not be on the side of God but in the receiver. When you allow other voices in life to interfere with God's voice, this is how you could miss what God is saying. Jesus said to take heed to what you hear (Mark 4:24).

The voices that are dominant in your life will be the ones that influence your choices and decisions. Consequently, you could miss the help God provides. Your new identity in Christ has made you a partner in God's ministration to people. Therefore, He wants you to hear His transmissions clearly, to help you do exactly what He wants. Jesus did exactly His Father's will.

• Living as an Effective Receiver

God wants you to have an increasing capacity to receive and follow through with His help or the motivations He works in your inner self. How can you make yourself an effective receiver? God says in Romans 12:1-2 to offer your body to Him as a living and holy sacrifice. Under the old dispensation, the sacrificial sheep burns on the altar of sacrifice. Understand that to offer your body as a holy sacrifice is to offer the members of your body to God.

When you offer your body as a living sacrifice to God, you burn but you live. God burns off some things in your life that diminish your ability to will and do what pleases Him. It makes room for your ability to receive and carry through God's motivations or His work in you.

Your inner motivations drive your daily life issues and deeds, such as behaviors and attitudes, which defines your relationship with people and the things of this world. The things people do or refuse to do originate from their inner motivations. The approach to marriage, business, handling of contracts or promises to people, and responses to personal and interpersonal issues are from inner motivations. Oftentimes, these inner motivations enhance or diminish the approach some people have towards the Christian life.

What do you love to see? What things do you love to speak in your conversations with people, even within yourself? What do you allow in your thought processes? What are the things you allow into your ears? What are the places you love to visit—either on the internet or in the physical? Some of these things could diminish your ability to please God. If you seriously offer your body to God, then He will build some spiritual and natural qualities in your inner being. You gain the spiritual ability to test and discern the will of God. You will discover that God's will is good, acceptable, and perfect for you.

LESSON: *To conform to the world is to become a slave to the god of this world. A slave obeys the master. Therefore, conformation to the world is to play by the same rules and do the very things the god of the world demand of you.*

Maximum benefit from God's help comes through a life of obedience. He says do not conform to the world but be transformed by renewing your mind. The mind renews by obeying God's Word. The Bible says in Romans 6:16 (KJV), "Know ye not, that to whom ye yield yourselves servants to obey, his servants ye are to whom ye obey; whether of sin unto death, or of obedience unto righteousness?" When you master the life of righteousness through obedience, it grows you in the life of holiness (Romans 6:19).

You grow in godliness if you daily yield to the Christ within you. If you do, you take on His godly attitudes. The Bible says, "Christ in you the hope of glory" (Colossians 1:27b). Learn to behold Christ through His Word and the Spirit of the Lord will take you through a transforming processes into the image of Christ, from one degree of glory to another (2 Corinthians 3:18).

Be determined to live by the new law that gives you the victory over the corruption in the world. It is the law of the Spirit of life in Christ Jesus. The world is under the power of the law of sin and death, which disables people's ability to submit to God; but you are a conqueror through the one by whom you have a new identity and power of His Kingdom.

• Sharpening Your Mind to Understand God's Will

The mind is spiritual in nature and the spirit of the mind functions as the compass of the mind into the things of God. If the spirit of your mind is renewed and your life transforms in ways God desires, you will understand God—who is Spirit and find His will for your life. You do not have to flip-flop between the spirit and the flesh. If that is happening in your life, check if your mind is really renewing!

The spirit perfectly understands the natural but the natural cannot comprehend the spiritual. God is Spirit. Therefore, to discern and understand the things of God, His ways and His will, the spirit of your mind must renew and become spiritual. When your mind becomes spiritual, you will understand that it is the will of God to pursue the attributes of who you have become in Christ. In fact, you will understand the value of your identity in Christ.

The spirit of your mind renews because you sincerely submit to the spirit and life of God's Word. As the spirit of your mind is renewing, you begin to comprehend and accept the validity of God's Word and allow it to influence your daily life issues. God created man to live by His Word. Unfortunately, it is not true with many people in the world…but not you, a born-again believer. You cannot go without the Word of God. You allow the Word to define your daily choices and decisions.

When the Holy Spirit brings God's Word to your mind, do not ignore it. Test if it is a word that will lead you into a lifestyle of presumption and deception and if not, act on it. As part of the new covenant enacted through Jesus, God wants to put His law within you, and write it on your heart (Jeremiah 31:33).

LESSON: *It is not just enough to claim to believe the Word of God, but also to allow it to define your decisions and choices in your life issues. It will orient the spirit of the mind for renewal because the mind not renewed will not provide protection against the affinities of the old self.*

Your Christian life is like climbing a steep staircase. It is tiring going up, but because you renew the spirit of your mind, you know the benefits of your endurance. You refuse hidden deeds of the flesh and inner attitudes that could eat you up spiritually. These inner attitudes and deeds could cause you to stagnate or step down from the upward match. It denies you the opportunity to walk in the power of your new identity in Christ. The power of your identity is the power of Christ's Kingdom residing in you. It is the Holy Spirit. The anointing of His presence destroys yokes that are not of Christ.

LESSON: *Strength and stability in the Christian life is not dependent just on the abundance of biblical knowledge. Rather, it is dependent on the knowledge that you allow to transform your mind. A transformed mind will lead to a transformed heart.*

The anointing of your identity is able to help you overcome the worldly ideas of right and wrong. It helps you overcome the "push and pull" of the flesh. The more your life heads toward your destiny, the greater the spirit of your mind will renew. You will understand the call to separate from evils in this world. You also would understand the call to holiness and righteousness as He is. Therefore, do not only claim the attributes of your identity in Christ, but the spirit of your mind also must renew.

The level the spirit of your mind has renewed will determine the level your mind becomes spiritual. Because you take delight and treasure God's Word, He gives you understanding as a blessing. For God's Word to renew the spirit of your mind, take note of the following:

- Live a diligent life of consistent Bible study and prayer. Make up your mind to define your life issues by the Word of God you know.
- Acknowledge your identity in Christ and understand the demands it places on your daily life and lifestyle.
- Learn and practice truth and righteousness as a lifestyle.
- Acknowledge you are no longer your own but Christ's. Christ died for you, so you no longer live for yourself but for Him who for your sake died and rose again.
- Let your view of life become more kingdom-minded. Since God is able to make all things work for your good, view and approach life with a positive attitude. Think on things that are true, honorable, just, pure, lovely, commendable, excellent, and praiseworthy.
- Treasure your new self or identity in Christ to help you set your mind on things above, where God has seated you with Christ.

To maintain a consistent growth in the spirit of your mind, refuse to conform to your former passions, when you were ignorant of your identity in Christ. See yourself as a king/queen and view certain lifestyles as beneath your dignity!

The Unseen Bridge

There is a spiritual bridge between your ability to put off your old self and to put on the new self. This bridge is the "spirit of the mind". The spirit of the mind is intangible, but powerful, to lead your life in ways that please God if it is renewed. The spirit of the mind is vulnerable to change by what you feed it.

For the spirit of the mind to renew, make the road along this "bridge" a one-way. As you travel along the country, there are a few places where you come across bridges. Some of these bridges are under repair. Consequently, traffic moves along the bridge in alternating turns. One side of the traffic stops, while opposite traffic moves along the bridge, and vice versa. Suppose the opposite traffic stops indefinitely!

Because your mind is under repair, make the "way" leading away from your new mind an "Exit" and the "way" leading into your new mind "No Entry" for anything that belong to your old self. Anything that could diminish your new mind must have no entry. When you discover anything that belongs to your old self, it must exit. However, it is not as simple as it seems, it is warfare and requires diligence to renew the spirit of your mind. It calls on you to examine your life constantly. In addition, learn to practice the encouragement in Philippians 4:8. That way, you can identify any fleshly or negative thoughts that cannot help renew your mind.

God wants you to set your thoughts on whatever are true, whatever is honorable, and whatever is just, whatever is pure, whatever is lovely, and whatever is commendable. Focus your mind on what is excellent, and what is worthy of praise. Then, practice what you know from God's Word. God has wonderfully made the human frame such that, whatever you focus on, can transform you.

Some Benefits of a Renewed Mind

A mind that is renewed or renewing is able to discern and understand God's demand for your identity in Christ. The Bible says you can test and know the perfect will of God for you (Romans 12:2). If your mind is renewing or being renewed, some of the following will be evident in your life:

- Your words change and become honorable and godly. You become truthful, righteous, and purposeful.
- Your thought processes change. You will think wholesome thoughts. You begin to think God thoughts, which grow the mind of Christ on the inside of you. Your understanding of God's ways grows.
- Your life of humility becomes sustainable. You do not fake humility but you live it. Your Master Jesus said He was meek and lowly, a character trait that He wants you to learn and live.
- You learn to love people irrespective of gender or ethnic origin. You learn to not fake love. Faking love is to show an outward sign of love contrary to what goes on in the heart.

- You gain a measure of understanding of God's ways and the knowledge of His presence with you. It motivates a life of righteousness and truth.
- A renewed mind helps you understand God's willingness to help you in your difficult times and seasons. It helps you endure in difficult times, trusting God to give you breakthrough.
- A renewed mind helps you identify corruptible things and ways of the world. It helps you avoid them. You are able to test the things that drive your daily life, whether they are of God or not.
- A renewed mind helps you escape the temptation to redefine the demands of your Christian life. In doing so, many get themselves into lifestyles and mindsets that diminish the power of their new identity in Christ.

Chapter 8
Power to Overcome Anxiety

Jesus said in Matthew 26:41, "Watch and pray, so that you will not fall into temptation. The spirit is willing, but the flesh is weak." To watch is to keep spiritually awake so that you can see any and everything that seeks to intrude into your life or catch any Christian principle you may be giving up. You keep watch so that nothing will sneak into your life by getting you to open a door for anxiety to engulf your mind and heart.

Some Understanding of Life

Someone said that life is a theater! How true! It is a theater because the "viewers" do not know what happens in the next scene. That is what produces the excitement of being there to watch. Life is never going to be free from unexpected events in its different times and seasons. As long as the "Repairer of the Bridge," Jesus Christ, has not returned, your life at one time or another will come face-to-face with some of the bumps and bruises in this life. No matter how careful you are, the bumps do sometimes come.

There are seasons when storms come to you unexpectedly. The world system in which we live is not perfect yet, so things do not always work as you expect. Only in God is there certainty! His Word of promise brings certainty to your life because not an iota of God's Word of promise will ever return to Him void. Its purpose is to accomplish what He has promised. Because you have an identity in Christ, let God's Word become the source of your confidence and your way of handling the unexpected occurrences in this life.

You may hear news of an unexpected health problem of a friend or family member, you may face significant challenges in your marriage, or your bump could be the loss of a job, which brings unexpected financial constraints on you or your family budget. All these have the tendency to impose on your heart fears about the future. These unexpected events are not preceded by an expected "arrival date"—giving you time to prepare. They just come upon you without warning. The sad part is that it imposes on your mind an imaginary video of your fears, showing you the worst-case scenario.

Jesus said to watch! What do you watch for? When a hired security guard watches a property or a house, he knows that there is the possibility of someone sneaking into the compound to steal something. Because the security guard has an awareness of the possibility of the unexpected, he has contingency plans, written or mental, to deal with the situation if it occurs.

God has given you the tools to understand that life has unexpected happenings. He has given you His Spirit to help you live with a vigilant heart and mind. When unexpected things happen, it does not have to take your heart and mind into the realm of worry and doubt. Trust God's ability to take care of you! Learn to declare what God's Word says about your situation! God has promised to hasten to perform what you say from His Word. If you doubt God's ability to take care of your difficult situation, you could slip into anxiety.

When God says He is faithful, you have to be convinced that He is. You God's own and He will not let what you cannot bear come in your life (1 Corinthians 10:13). With what He allows, He also provides the help you need to go through it unscratched spiritually. God can replace material things that you lose. God cares about your spiritual stand in Christ; therefore, He will take care of your life difficulties. He wants to see you rooted and established in Christ no matter what challenges may come into your life.

Anxiety will find it difficult to create a "room" in your heart or mind if you establish yourself mentally in your trust in Christ. When you watch, you look for occurrences, events, and life issues that could disorient your mind and heart to respond negatively, causing you to open doors to the spirit of anxiety. You must also watch to deny anxiety especially after you have offered your prayers to God. This is very important when God's answer to your needs seem to delay. Remember, anxiety can be hurtful and destructive.

Ask God to give you an understanding of your identity in Christ and of His ways. Be convinced that you are His, and His overwhelming power is ready to help you in every one of your life situations.

God planned solutions to your life problems from the foundation of all things. Therefore, do not let anxiety be the reason you fail to advance into His divine goodness and purposes. He says to you to not fear what the world fears nor be in dread (Isaiah 8:12b). God wants His peace (and not fear) to rule in your heart; this is one of His callings for your life in Christ. He wants you to be thankful in all circumstances (Colossians 3:15).

LESSON: *For an effective life of victory over anxiety in life issues, always look for something good in the haystack of confusion. Let that capture your imagination and focus so you can thank the Lord for it and for victory over the confusion.*

Anxiety and Faith

Anxiety works the same way as faith. Unfortunately, anxiety thrives on negative hopes. It is faith in the negative direction. In anxiety, your negative hope causes you to be apprehensive. Sometimes, it can cause you to experience a nervous breakdown. Unlike faith, where you expect something good to happen for you, in anxiety, you fear that something bad could happen in your life situation. If left unchecked, this fear could become very strong and will take over your meditations.

LESSON: *Fear in your life situation is spiritual approval of the negative things that Satan wants to bring to pass in your life.*

Since the things you fear could happen are not real or visible, it makes anxiety a negative hope. It is unbelief. The spirit of anxiety has destroyed many people because, left unchecked, it sent them down into depression. A sustained state of anxiety will raise your blood pressure, which oftentimes, have destructive consequences.

I have a friend who was very anxious about so many things due to her past actions and behaviors, and she thought something bad could happen to her. In the Christian life, it is very important to be realistic. When you sin, face up to it, accept your wrongdoing, and ask God for forgiveness. When you fail to confess your sins to God, you give opportunity to the devil to oppress your mind and heart with guilt. When you have confessed, you deny the mind and heart the opportunity to live in your past.

LESSON: *Usually, your anxiety level is dependent on the level of your trust and belief in God. If you lack trust and belief in God, you are likely to have a frequent visitation by the spirit of anxiety and impatience.*

Called to the Deep

God is giving you a kingdom (Hebrews 12:28). It is inexcusable for you not to ask God for an inner revelation of His sovereign and overwhelming power. This way, you can grow a deeper knowledge of His presence with you, even in times and seasons of problems. The unbeliever may lack the knowledge of God's ability, but not you. Jesus said you have been given to know the mysteries of the Kingdom of Heaven (Matthew 13:11).

To know the mysteries of the Kingdom, embed your life and your trust in the King of the Kingdom. There, you see yourself as a coworker with Him. In fact, God wants you to participate in His divine nature. This is how your knowledge grows of yourself as a coworker with Him. Your heart will understand that His business is yours and your business, including all of your life issues, is His. You will then become convinced of His Almighty power, which is available and ready to help you. Such knowledge will strengthen your inner "walls" against anxiety. Your deep place in God will become a well in your inner self to help you overcome many anxiety-generating issues that confront you in this world.

Elisha and His Servant

The story of Elisha and his servant is a typical example of dwelling in the deeper place in God. The Syrian king realized that Elisha was revealing the secrets of their plans to the children of Israel. The king of Syria sent horses, chariots, and a great army to go capture Elisha. The servant of Elisha rose in the morning and found their abode surrounded. This is the response of the servant recorded in 2 Kings 6:15, "Alas, my master! What shall we do?" Now, Elisha, living in the deep place in the God he served, prayed two simple prayers. He did not call the support of a prayer team or engage in long prayers.

Anxiety and apprehension overcame the servant, but not Elisha. To the servant, he and his master's lives were over. Unlike the servant, Elisha set his eyes on the multitude of angels ready to defend them. His calmness in the time of trouble, due to his deep-seated trust in God, gave him the right attitude of heart and mind to know exactly what to do. Two simple prayers did the job of deliverance.

LESSON: *Do you know God's angels with you are greater in number than the many problems that confront you? Are you aware that there are angels ready to respond to your declarations of faith in your time of trouble? Do not allow anxiety to take away your ability to declare a Word for God's angels to act on your behalf.*

Learn to stay deep in your Savior and learn to believe Him who is Almighty and overwhelming in power. Believe in His promises and do not let your mind and heart argue against them. Do not ignore or overlook His power to keep and help you in your times and seasons of need.

Let your confidence in God's ability help invigorate you to defy the ability of anxiety to take a piece of the godly meditations of your heart and mind. This way, you will be able to see life events, occurrences, and issues in their correct spiritual and natural perspectives. You will then be able to identify what is of God and what is not. Situations that seem uncertain will become clear to your understanding.

Anxiety—A Fleshly Inspiration and Mindset

Anxiety is a fleshly lifestyle and negative spiritual inspiration. It generates negative hope in your mind and heart contrary to your heart's desire. It can prevent you from receiving spontaneous, righteous thoughts or illuminations from the Holy Spirit in your time of trouble. Therefore, you have to see anxiety as an enemy, which can deprive you from walking in God's pleasure. Since anxiety generates negative hopes, it is faith in reverse. Faith develops from the convictions you have from God's Word and promises. Negative hope is therefore a lack of faith. The Bible says in Hebrews 11:6, "Without faith, it is impossible to please God."

LESSON: *Since anxiety produces negative hopes, why should you hope for what you do not want to happen in your time of need? Just think about this!*

Do not allow the fleshly part of your life to take precedence over your spiritual life. Set your mind so you can speak life into all your life situations. The fleshly mind cannot submit to God in times of need (Romans 8:6-8). Those who are in the flesh cannot please God. The mind controlled by anxiety is hostile to God because it fails to submit to God's ability to help.

The desires of the flesh are opposed to the desires of the Spirit. Consequently, anxiety, which is fleshly, denies you the ability to trust God in your uncertain life situations. When you feel overwhelmed by life challenges and demands, you then know that anxiety is seeking a way to come in your life. Confront it by prayer and supplication so you do not loose control of your mind.

Anxiety and the Unknown Spiritual Realm

God warns His people not to walk in the ways of the world. He wants them not to fear or dread what people of the world fear and dread (Isaiah 8:12). You do not allow fear to cause you to join an alliance with anything or anyone. Let the Word and God's purposes for you rule your life. The Bible says in 1 Corinthians 10:23, "All things are lawful, but not all things are helpful. All things are lawful, but not all things build up." Do not get yourself into things that could later cause anxiety to take a piece of your mind and heart.

In the case of my friend, she was having a hard time practicing the counsel I gave her. When anxiety thrives and left unchecked for a long time, it affects your outlook, your views, interpersonal relationships, and your approach to life issues. It slows your zest. When it does, it begins to affect you on your job, your relationship with your wife or husband, and your relationships with other people.

One day I saw my friend and immediately knew that she was at a crossroad situation. I told her she had better learn to trust the ability of God to help her or she could slip into depression. I asked her, "If you had the ability to change the events that make you anxious, would you change them?" She said to me, "Yes!" I said to her, then why do you destroy yourself for events you had no control over?

It is very important to understand that when you allow anxiety to thrive in your life, it will take the mind into an unknown place in the spiritual realm. There, the mind receives deceptive mental pictures and spontaneous thoughts about your situations and events. When the mind feeds the heart with such deceptive information, it produces more anxiety and worry; it gives you negative convictions, leading to careless actions. When anxiety activates negative convictions, it leads you to act in certain ways outside of God's will and out of His righteous boundaries.

Doris Example of Deceptive Inspiration

Doris was the wife of a successful, business executive who frequently left for days at a time on business tours. Because he did not talk very much, Doris became very suspicious and anxious that he was probably going after other women. In one particular week when the husband was on one of his trips, Doris could not sleep. She struggled to sleep, but because of her anxiety, sleep slipped away from her.

The few times that she was fortunate to dose off, she had many dreams. In one dream, she saw her husband in a place. Around him were three women. She immediately woke up from sleep. That was it! To Doris, the dream confirmed her presumed fears. Unfortunately, the dream was born out of her anxious mind and heart. It brought her spirit to an unknown place where she received this deceptive dream.

You will not believe what Doris did next… she took the phone and called her husband deep in the night. Overcome by the spirit of impatience, she started railing condemnations on the husband, how despicable he was in what he was doing. The lack of trust for her husband eventually broke up the marriage.

LESSON: *Do not allow your anxious mind and heart to drive you to that place in the spiritual realm where you could be deceived by deceptive dreams and visions.*

Anxiety does not only take hold of your mind when you face an uncertain consequence of your wrongdoing in life issues. At other times, anxiety can take hold of your mind when you fail to trust God's ability to take care of your uncertain life situation. In addition, anxiety can take hold of your mind if you very often allow the fears of your tomorrow take hold of your heart. When allowed to thrive, anxiety will produce frustration, impatience, and depression.

Frustration, Impatience and Anxiety

Usually, frustration is born out of unfulfilled expectations. When frustration takes root in your life, it causes you to be impatient. Since frustration and impatience are the offspring of anxiety, they rule the heart. Nevertheless, it is an indication of a lack of trust and faith in the Word of God. Trust and faith in God is born out of inner conviction of His faithfulness to help you in the times of difficulties.

I believe you are a believer who knows your calling and identity in Christ, and you believe in His soon return. Therefore, the Bible calls on you to be sober-minded. With a sober mind, you are able to stay patient in life issues and events. Consequently, you do not hurry yourself into things that eventually could cause you anxiety. In addition, with a sober mind, patience will rule in your heart. Then you can watch so you do not get yourself weighted down by life's business. Impatience and frustration can cause you to overlook the doors the Lord creates for your solutions.

Impatience will show up in your responses to life challenges and could cause you to presume a thing is good or that there is an eminent danger when it is actually false. It is a sign that anxiety has taken hold of the heart.

Therefore, anxiety is an action kicker, which can motivate you to act outside of spiritual common sense.

Impatience causes many people, including some Christians, to make careless decisions, choices, and actions. For example, when you have prayed about your needs or uncertain life issues and circumstances, impatience could cause you sometimes to draw false conclusions. This is especially true when the answer to your prayers delays. Other times, impatience could cause you to go before the Lord in prayer with your mind already made-up. When that happens, you open yourself up to the deceiver to deceive with a voice or confirm what is in your mind.

Chapter 9
Some Weapons for Dealing with Anxiety

Now you know that anxiety is lack of faith in the God who says that without faith no one can please Him. You also know that anxiety is a fleshly and negative spiritual inspiration. Therefore, you have to find every weapon available to overcome it. First, you have to identify God's hand in your challenging and troubled times, then, you can yield to Him and say, "Lord, I do not know what is going on in my life, but my eyes are on you".

Your next step is to maintain an attitude of thanksgiving. This attitude usually activates God's response: to take over the responsibility of calming your mind and heart in your situation. He will respond with His mighty hand of deliverance. Then you and people around you will come to know your God, for He alone is God! So let your attitude in the midst of your challenges bring glory to God.

• Thanksgiving

In every life situation that you experience, thanksgiving should never be far from your lips, even in your moments of challenges. Thanksgiving will orient your mind and heart correctly to the spiritual and natural aspects of your situation. Consequently, your attitude towards your problem will change and you will learn to focus on the Word of God and His promises rather than the fears. Soon, your mind and heart will grasp exactly what the Holy Spirit is leading you to do for your breakthrough.

LESSON: *If you learn to focus on the promises of God in your time of trouble, your mind becomes clear so you can receive divine inspiration to the solution for your problems.*

Thanksgiving helps keep your mind clear of worries and anxieties, so you can see how events unfold, and the direction the Holy Spirit provides for your victory. It also gives you insight into how God handles situations in your life.

No matter what comes in your life to cause problems and difficulties, God has a solution for every one of them. He planned the solution to your life situations before the foundation of the earth. He knew the time you would become His own through Christ.

One may ask, "If God knows everything, why doesn't He prevent certain situations?" How nice if God would prevent all our life difficulties. Understand that you have a will, and you oftentimes do some things in life without consulting with the Source of your new life. Consequently, things happen in your life and temptations follow. Nevertheless, in all that, God's loving presence will not allow these things to destroy you, except you could go through some pain. He said in 1 Corinthians 10:13, "No temptation has taken you but what is common to man; but God is faithful, who will not allow you to be tempted above what you are able, but with the temptation also will make a way to escape, so that you may be able to bear it." This is the reason you have to overcome anxiety so you can find the way of escape.

• Rejoicing and Praises

To grasp the power of rejoicing, convince yourself of the existence and the reality of the God you serve. Convince yourself He cares for you and He rewards those who diligently seek Him.

The last time I met the friend that I previously referred to, I saw anxiety written all over her face. So I said to her, "Rejoice in the Lord always; again I will say, rejoice," quoting Philippians 4:4. She said to me, "How can I rejoice when my life seems like I am in the middle of a raging fire?" I said to her, "When the Lord commanded us to rejoice, He did not specify when to do so and when not to do so! He said to rejoice in Him always." The Lord, through Apostle Paul, gave this command to rejoice with emphasis, "Again I say rejoice!" Rejoicing is a very powerful spiritual weapon that many fail to grasp.

King David gained some insights into God's ability to help in all seasons. He said in Psalms 23:5, "You prepare a table before me in the presence of my enemies; You anoint my head with oil; my cup overflows". King David also said in the same verse that God is able to anoint your head with oil of gladness and make your cup run over. A cup runs over only when it contains more than it can hold. In anxiety, you run yourself "dry" spiritually and deny others to see God's glory in your life. When you rejoice in the midst of your problems, it gives glory to God. In addition, people around you will know that the God you serve is your present helper in your time of trouble.

If God sets a table before you in the presence of your enemies, you do not allow the enemy of anxiety to keep your head down when the Lord is inviting you to a feast. You are the planting of the Lord. Keep your head up so you can see the "table" the Lord has set before you for your triumph over the enemy of anxiety. You cannot have a feast set before you and continue to engage in your pity party, with mourning and groaning in your heart. The anointing of the Lord breaks yokes and chains (Isaiah 10:27).

Suppose in the natural, you always use profit sharing from your company to pay some bills. Unfortunately, you hear there will not be profit sharing this year. You became so upset with yourself and anxious about what that means for your mounting bills. Usually, a company party will precede the profit sharing. No profit sharing, there will be no party. Suddenly, the company calls employees to a profit-sharing party. Would you continue to be anxious and sad because your company is not going to have profit sharing? Your boss would wonder about your mental or emotional state. He will say to you, "What is wrong with you? What are you worrying about?"

• Trust God

Do not be anxious, God is with you! Jesus said, "Have faith in God." He also said in Matthew 6:34, "Therefore do not be anxious about tomorrow, for tomorrow will be anxious for itself. Sufficient for the day is its own trouble." God wants you to trust Him with every one of the things that causes you anxiety and to learn to rejoice. He will anoint you with the oil of gladness instead of mourning, and a garment of praise instead of a faint spirit (Isaiah 61:3). Then you can rejoice in the presence of your enemies, your problems, and fears. God wants the whole world to see you as an oak of righteousness and the planting of the Lord, that He may be glorified.

Your identity in Christ comes with God's powerful anointing to help you break free from yokes of slavery, even anxiety. You have to orient your heart and mind to walk in the attributes of your identity. Then you will become fully equipped to overcome the yoke of anxiety.

Anxiety drags many to depression and destruction if permitted to thrive. In its slavery, you are motivated to see the things that cause anxiety greater than focusing on the God whom you serve. It makes you think fleshly thoughts. Fleshly thinking will fail to trust God's ability to help because it defines life situations by negative convictions. Anxiety is your enemy; so do not permit it to thrive in your heart and mind. Cast it down with God's Word.

LESSON: *Let your knowledge of God's anointing on you motivate you to speak to your mountains of troubles and see the hand of the Almighty God keep you protected from anxiety.*

When you rejoice in your time and season of problems and difficulties, you defy the forces seeking to draw you into anxiety. The walls of the city of Jericho fell flat after the children of Israel marched around the city for seven days and seven times on the seventh day. After the final march, the priests blew their trumpets very loud and the people gave a great shout (Joshua 6:2-5).

What I say to you are not religious theories but are practical spiritual exercises God wants you to practice, so you will experience its power and effects. When you have prayed that the yokes of your problems be broken, learn to shift to rejoicing.

You see, very often, some people want everything to line up with their expectations before they obey God's command to rejoice. That is not what God is saying to you and me. He said rejoice always! That means you do so with or without problems. The God who created you and I knows the spiritual power inherent in rejoicing. As I said earlier, it is a very powerful spiritual weapon.

Simply put, suppose a lion has entered your countryside house and the only barrier between you and death is a door. The lion is behind the door because it can smell your presence. You will not wait until the lion leaves the house before you shout for help. You will shout at the top of your longs to get people's attention of the your very precarious situation. Therefore, shout and rejoice in the presence of your troubles!

• God's Prescription

Jesus said in the world you will have troubles but He says to you, "Take heart, I have overcome the world" (John 16:33). It is a known fact that life in this world comes with troubles. There is no doubt about that! Nevertheless, Jesus, the One who holds your life, says, "Peace I leave with you; My peace I give to you. Not as the world gives do I give to you. Let not your hearts be troubled, neither let them be afraid" (John 14:27).

Why is Jesus saying this to you? Jesus knows the challenges men face in this flesh and blood. He has tasted it. The Bible says, "For we do not have a High Priest who is unable to sympathize with our weaknesses, but One who in every respect has been tempted as we are, yet without sin" (Hebrews 4:15).

Jesus knows the troubles you will face in this life, and the times you will be tempted to yield to anxieties.

Jesus knows what lies ahead of your today and of your tomorrow. He commands you in Philippians 4:6, not be anxious about anything, but in everything let God know your requests through prayer, supplication, and thanksgiving. If God says do not be anxious about anything, He means that to include EVERYTHING. However, can you and I rule over anxiety? Anxiety of the child of God is an insult to His overwhelming power to provide and protect.

The fact that God says, "Do not be anxious", is an indication He has given you what you need to reign over anxiety. It is very interesting God says to thank Him after you have prayed and offered your supplications before Him. This is where God needs your cooperation so He can help you. Because you do what He commands you, His peace, which surpasses all understanding, will guard your heart and your mind in Christ Jesus (Philippians 4:6-7). This way, you can laugh in your storms.

Whenever you visit the doctor with your physical problems, you narrate how you feel in your body. Then the doctor will prescribe any appropriate medication for you to take. It is your responsibility to go buy the medication and then take the course of the medication as instructed on the box or bottle. When you do, your physical problem does not go away in a single day. However, as you keep on taking the medication, you get well eventually.

As I indicated earlier in Chapter 6 and other places in this book, I want you to realize that Philippians 4:8 is God's prescription to help you overcome anxiety. Like a natural prescription, take the full course of God's prescription. This is so important because anxiety is like a monster. It takes hold of your mind and refuses to let you go free. Therefore, you have to confront it with God's prescription. In every one of your life problems, difficulties, or needs, God wants you to think wholesome thoughts as He prescribes to you in Philippians 4:8.

Apply Faith in Uncertain Times

God commands you in Philippians 4:8 not to focus on the negative aspects of occurrences and events around you, even in your life situations. When the report came from Jairus' house that his daughter was dead, what was Jesus' response? He said Jairus' daughter was not dead but sleeping (Mark 5:39-42).

Jesus knew the girl was dead. However, that was not His expectation. His faith conviction was that the girl would live again. Therefore, He was not anxious about what had happened. He could have beaten Himself for the consequence for His delay.

Jesus was calm and did not say what the people were saying. He spoke His convictions of faith. The girl was dead! That was the reality. However, Jesus' faith conviction says she was sleeping and He went to wake her up. He received His convictions.

Refuse to flood your mind with the grim side of your uncertain life issues and situations. Then you will deny anxiety a place in your mind and heart. You do not have to let down your belief in God. Probably Jairus came to Jesus full of anxiety; what could possibly be happening to the child while Jesus was doing other things along the way to his house. His fear was confirmed when he was told the child was dead, 'Why bother the teacher, your daughter is dead.' Jesus said to Jairus, "Do not fear, only believe".

LESSON: The a*bility to defy fears in uncertain times is one of the difficult things for some people to do, even some Christians. Such Christians seem to act outside of all they have been taught.*

Daily, people contend with uncertainties in this world, some of which produce anxieties. Nevertheless, Jesus says to all, as He said to Jairus, "Do not fear, only believe". To see the bright side of every uncertain life situation, you have to learn to take God's prescription in Philippians 4:8. Let it immunize you spiritually against intrusion of the spirit of anxiety.

Sometimes, you immunize yourself by taking injections to prevent catching a disease or sickness. Therefore, learn to take God's prescription not only in your troubled times but more so in your good times. It will create a spiritual "wall" against anxiety. You have to learn to look at the good side of everything you go through in life. You will find something that can encourage you. Build on that and thank God for the victory.

Jesus Christ means everything God wants for your life. He is your surest and tested foundation whom you can trust in your life. God said in Isaiah 28:16, "Behold, I Am the One who has laid as a foundation in Zion, a stone, a tested stone, a precious cornerstone, of a sure foundation: 'Whoever believes will not be in haste.'"

Let your life testify of the greatness of the God in you. The Lord's return is at hand (Philippians 4:5). If you truly trust the God of your salvation, you will obey and take His prescription. It will fortify your mind against anxiety. Jesus will help you overcome anxiety. The Bible says in Hebrews 2:18, "For because He Himself has suffered when tempted, He is able to help those who are being tempted. You have to take these critical steps as written in Hebrews 4:16:

- Elevate your confidence in God your Father and helper.
- Draw near to the throne of grace in your times of trouble.
- Seek mercy from the God you trust.
- Ask for grace to help you overcome.

Then, take God's prescription as I indicated above.

LESSON: *If you have no savings in your bank account, you cannot withdraw money from the account. In like manner, build your faith and trust in God's Word, then in your day of trouble, you will have the confidence to approach the throne of grace. Do not become vulnerable to the spirit of anxiety and impatience.*

Build a deep and a solid foundation of conviction in your God. Then, when days of adversity quiet your mouth, your deep inner trust in God will keep you from the anxiety that destroys many in the world.

LESSON: *It is not so much of shouting and outward show of charisma that proves your strength in the Lord. Let your deep roots of knowledge, trust, and faith in God keep you strong and steady in life's uncertainties.*

Biblical Examples of Victory over Anxiety

In Jericho, shouting in the form of worship brought down the fortified walls of the city for the children of Israel to overrun it. I will consider other examples below:

- **Abide in the Rock**

Jesus is a unique personality in God's system of things. He is the Rock of Ages! The Bible says He is the image of the invisible God, the firstborn of all creation. For by Him, God created all things in Heaven and on Earth, visible and invisible, whether thrones or dominions or rulers or authorities. God created all things through Jesus and for Him. He is before all things, and in Him, all things hold firmly together.

In addition, He is the head of the church. He is the firstborn from the dead, that in everything He might be preeminent. For in Him all the fullness of God was pleased to dwell, and through Him to reconcile to Himself all things, whether on earth or in Heaven, making peace by the blood of His cross (Colossians 1:15-20). The Bible says in Psalm 91:1, "He who dwells in the secret place of the Most High shall rest under the shadow of the Almighty"

Jesus said in John 15:6, "Abide in Me, and I in you. As the branch cannot bear fruit by itself, unless it abides in the vine, neither can you, unless you abide in Me." You abide in Jesus because He is your Rock, your fortress, and your deliverer (2 Samuel 22:2). He will deliver you from the intrusion of the spirit of anxiety because the joy of the Lord is your strength. The Lord says in Nehemiah 8:10b, "Do not be grieved, for the joy of the LORD is your strength." Joy, or rejoicing, is one of the weapons used to overcome anxiety.

• Apostle Paul and Silas Example

These two great evangelists were beaten and cast into prison because they cast out a spirit of divination from a girl the masters were using for profit. This happened in the city of Philippi. The jailor fastened their feet with iron chains. In the natural, this seemed to be a very sad situation. They had a very successful Holy Spirit-directed ministry to a group of women, won, and baptized a woman named Lydia. In the spiritual sense however, Paul and Silas did not see their situation as terrible or worry about what could happen the next day.

Around the midnight hour, Paul and Silas turned their prison cell into a worship session. They prayed and sang hymns to God, while the other prisoners listened to them. Suddenly, there was a violent earthquake, which shook the foundations of the prison. All the prison doors immediately flew open and every prison's chains broke off their feet (Acts 16:13-26). If you find yourself imprisoned by the spirit of anxiety, offer praise and worship to the Lord in ways you have never done, and see the "chains" break off your heart.

• Jehoshaphat's Example

In 2 Chronicles 20:21-22, a great multitude made up of the Moabites, Ammonites, Meunites, and others came against the land of Israel and there was no way of escape. Jehoshaphat was the king of Israel. In his fright, Jehoshaphat and the people sought help from the Lord and proclaimed a fast through all Judah. Read the prayer Jehoshaphat prayed to the Lord in his time of trouble. You may learn something from it. He did not pray this prayer before the trouble hit. He did so in the midst of the trouble.

Jehoshaphat said in 2 Chronicles 20:6-9,

"O LORD, God of our fathers, are You not God in Heaven, and do You not rule over all the kingdoms of the nations, and in Your hand is there not power and might, so that no one is able to withstand You? Are you not our God, who drove out the inhabitants of this land before Your people Israel, and gave it to the descendants of Abraham Your friend forever? And they dwell in it and have built You a sanctuary in it for Your name, saying, 'If disaster comes upon us— the sword, judgment, pestilence, or famine—we will stand before this temple and in Your presence (for Your name is in this temple), and cry out to You in our affliction, and You will hear and save.'"

Note that in his prayer, Jehoshaphat reminded God of who He is and the covenant they have made with Him in the past. He also reminded God what He had promised to do in their times of trouble. Then, he said something that triggered God's response. He said in 2 Chronicle 20:12, "O our God, will you not judge them? For we have no power against this great multitude that is coming against us, nor do we know what to do, but our eyes are on You." Today, you have a covenant with God through Jesus Christ. God says He will hear the prayer you pray in Jesus' name.

The words of Jehoshaphat in this verse are very significant to acknowledge. Do not be one of those who go to God in their times of trouble but inside, have alternate ways in mind to confront their situation. Jehoshaphat said, "We do not know what to do, but our eyes are on You".

LESSON: *In your time of trouble, let God know you have no alternative bridge to your solution except His help. Let Him know your eyes are on Him and Him alone.*

The Lord said to Jehoshaphat in 2 Chronicles 20:15, "Do not be afraid nor dismayed because of this great multitude, for the battle is not yours, but God's." God went on to say, "You will not need to fight in this battle. Stand firm, hold your position, and see the salvation of the Lord on your behalf" (2 Chronicles 20:17).

Because you have an identity in Christ, God says to you when you confront life situations that could produce anxiety, "The battle is not yours". Pray and stand firm; hold your position of trust and confidence in God's promises. If you think you fight your battles alone, you may likely allow anxiety in your heart. Remain in your position of trust, and you will soon see the salvation of your God.

Because he was convinced of God's ability to fulfill His promises, Jehoshaphat did what the world today would call crazy. He appointed singers to go before the army, praising the Lord in holy attire. As they went before the army they sang, "Give thanks to the Lord, for His steadfast love endures forever". While they praised, the Lord set an ambush against the large army that came against Judah, so that they were overthrown and they slaughtered one another (2 Chronicle 20:21-22). You serve this God and He wants to show Himself strong in your behalf if you would hold your position of trust and not allow anxiety to beat you down.

LESSON: *Learn to add praises to the list of your emergency actions in times and events that could cause you anxiety. Use the "Jehoshaphat method"—sing praises to the God who has created your identity in Christ.*

You are God's own and He has promised to deliver you in your times of trouble. Do not think you have to do so much in your challenging times. All that time, you are missing the still small voice of the Holy Spirit saying to you, "Be still, and know I Am God".

Jehoshaphat replaced his anxiety with songs of praise and worship. Catch the revelation of God's ability to help you in your times and seasons when nothing else can; times when you do not know what to do. The lesson in 2 Chronicles 20 teaches you to learn to pray using the right words before your God in your times of trouble. Do not pray a prayer that shows your frustration and anxiety. You are encouraged to let everyone know your forbearance, your restraint, or your self-control (Philippians 4:5). You cannot obey this verse when anxiety is all over your heart and mind!

What is your demeanor when life situations appear frightening? You have to remember your identity in the One who calmed the Sea. He will come with His overwhelming power, or like Moses at the Red Sea, He will tell you to "stretch out the authority" He has given you. He wants you to use His authority in life situations that deviates from His divine purpose for you and your environment.

Learn some Strategies

In life, you normally learn some principles and strategies that help you overcome many life situations. In the Lord, you have to learn some spiritual principles or strategies to help you stand strong in this turbulent world and to avoid getting your heart and mind always spinning with anxieties. I will elaborate on a few of the spiritual principles below:

- Refuse to allow negative thoughts and expectations to capture your heart. Remember what I referred to in Chapter 6 as the "Job factor". Job's words revealed thoughts that he allowed to capture his imaginations. He said the things that he feared the most had come upon him, and what he dreaded had befallen him. Job lived with a negative expectation of something bad happening to him.

- Never allow delay (concerning any of God's promises) to keep you out of alignment with His work in your life.
- Grow your vigilance, stability, and faithfulness to God in season and out of season, when no one is watching you.
- Build your confidence in His Word of promise in your daily life experiences.
- Learn to remain diligent, and always keep your spiritual receptors on in life situations.
- Watch so you can identify and confess any wrongdoing that could possibly open your mind and heart's doors to anxiety. So long as you live in your body and in this corrupt world, anxiety will seek to gain entrance into your life. Therefore, learn to watch, praying in every season, that you may have the strength to escape all the anxiety-causing issues in this life.
- Do not allow the world's system of acceptable and unacceptable things in life situations become the measure or standard that you use for yourself. Allow God's Word to become the standard for your life. If you fail to do so, failure of the world's system will mean your failure.
- Do not place yourself in life situations that could cause you to do things that would later torment your mind and heart with anxieties.
- What do you have to do in this world full of anxiety? Equip yourself with the full armor of God so you can withstand any attempt of life to invade your heart and mind with anxiety. Also, grow strong in your conviction of God's Word and promises.
- In each of your life situations, you have to ask yourself questions such as the following:

  o If God had said what He says in His Word about my situation, will He fail if I trust Him?
  o Is there any written record where God failed those who trusted Him?
  o Is 1 Corinthians 10:13 true in my current situation? The answer is always, "God never fails". So do not cloud your heart with anxiety. Rather, look for the way out!

Be confident that your God has power to deal with all life issues that could cause anxiety in your heart or in mind. If God allows anything in your life, know that He is up to something good for you. Get closer to Him, be still, and listen for a way through your situation. Do not be anxious about anything. The Lord's return is soon, so live with a clear and sound mind and heart so you can pray in every life situation. Always remember that the power of God's Kingdom dwells in you. Apply it in your uncertain life situation, declaring His Word of promise.

Chapter 10
Sustaining the Fire of Identity: The Presence of God

There are dimensions of the presence of God in the world and with you. His presence is everywhere and He is a witness to all that goes on amongst the children of men. Nothing in this world escapes His scrutiny. Another dimension of God's presence has to do with individual people. This presence of God brings divine blessings to these individuals. However, God's presence in such individuals comes with responsibilities they learn to fulfill. I will consider some of these responsibilities and blessings later in this chapter.

Acknowledge the Presence of God

Your life daily confronts needs and sometimes challenges. Every person has things that pose challenges. You live one life in the current world. If you know that God is everywhere, then you have to acknowledge you live in His presence. Whether or not life is treating you well, the knowledge of God's presence will influence your every life challenge or problem.

Some of your life challenges energize you to seek more of God's presence because you know that in His presence, you can go through anything without unfaithfulness to Him. The victory God gives you becomes a catalyst, which strengthens your knowledge of His presence with you. Therefore, in the heat of your life pursuits and difficulties, always remind yourself of the presence and eyes of God on you.

God's presence with you activates the resurrection power in your life. How invigorating to know that the power that raised Jesus Christ from the dead works for you. It works for you and through you because God's presence is with you. Your responsibility is to stay fired up daily, not allowing anything or any lifestyles to diminish God's presence with you. He is a holy God!

The knowledge of your identity in Christ will become a source of inspiration to help you desire a deeper relationship with God through Christ Jesus. As I indicated earlier, God wants you closer because you have His identity. In addition, He has invested His Spirit in you and washed your soul with the blood of Jesus. God wants you to deny the world's corruptible things that defile body and spirit. It diminishes people's ability to enjoy God's presence and the power it provides. I want to reiterate that corruption is anything you do in life that diminishes your spiritual status in Christ Jesus.

LESSON: *In every season of your life, with or without challenges or problems, never lose the knowledge that your God is with you. Let that give you the confidence to stand strong, irrespective of what you go through in life.*

God's promise of His presence with you is a sure promise! The God you serve has decreed in Genesis 8:22, "While the earth remains, seedtime, and harvest, cold and heat, summer and winter, day and night, shall not cease". He has promised you His presence (Matthew 28:20). If Genesis 8:22 fails, then the promises God has made concerning your life in Christ can also fail. He says in Matthew 24:35, "Heaven and earth will pass away, but My words will not pass away". Because you love Him, His promise to you will not fail! Your identity in Christ Jesus makes Him your only source and dependency in life. Your obedience to Jesus' Word will motivate Him and His Father to come into residence in you (John 14:22-23).

As you desire God's presence with you, also desire to live in His presence. To live in the presence of God does not imply you go and kneel down somewhere and pray. It includes much prayer, but to live in the presence of God is a mental orientation. You acknowledge His presence with you in all your life issues. Therefore, you learn to orient your heart to a life of truth, humility, righteousness, and holiness, all through obedience. You learn to deny ungodliness and worldly lust. Regard God's presence with you like the CEO of your company, who comes into your office while you work. Because you know the CEO is present in your office, you cut out all foolishness and all unprofessional activities and jokes.

Apostle Paul acknowledged God's presence in his life and he said in Romans 8:31, "who can be against us?" To all who depend on God, the Bible encourages to cast all your cares on Him because He cares for you. God has power to exalt you because you yield and humble your heart to obey what He says to you (1 Peter 5:6-7).

Hunger for More of God's Presence

To hunger for more of the presence of God is to seek more of the presence of the Holy Spirit in your life. In fact, it is growing in the attributes of your identity in Christ Jesus, which is a life of godliness, righteousness, and holiness—all through obedience. The holy people of God did not live carelessly. Those who touched God's heart were "broken" before Him and consequently, lived lives of righteousness, godliness, and holiness.

LESSON: *To desire more of the presence of God and yet subscribe to a careless lifestyle that ignores holiness, righteousness, and godliness is a deceptive life.*

The psalmist wrote, "As the deer pants for the water brooks, So pants my soul for You, O God. My soul thirsts for God, for the living God. When shall I come and appear before God?" (Psalm 42:1-2). In verse three of this psalm, the psalmist wrote, "My tears have been my food day and night, While they say to me, "Where is your God?"" This attitude is a depiction of a person who ignores what people say, as he/she strives to satisfy the hunger for the presence of God.

Oftentimes, the dear will travel over treacherous terrains to get to a stream, where it can quench its thirst. Like the deer, you have to learn to defy people's demeaning words so you would press in to seek more of the presence of your God.

God assures you in Jeremiah 29:13, "And you will seek Me and find Me, when you search for Me with all your heart". God knows when you diligently seek Him and you walk in the attributes of your new identity in Christ. However, it oftentimes seems as though you feel for something unattainable, but that is how it works for all. God is invisible and we all do feel or grope for Him in one way or another. It is however, very satisfying for all the people who seek God. He monitors your heart and has promised to withhold no good thing from you and will bestow favor and honor on you (Psalm 84:11). The young lion suffers want and hunger; but those who seek the Lord lack no good thing (Psalm 34:10).

In your quest for more of God's presence with you, learn not to give up walking in the attributes of your new self. No believer can go to any "depth" with God if he or she is not hungry for more of truth, righteousness, and faithfulness. The key to success in this Christian life is obedience. You obey God because you defy the lies of the world that it is not possible to "touch" God through the power of His Spirit in you.

The decision to obey God is a choice left to each believer to fulfill. Once you make this choice, you have all the resources of God to help you through the difficult times and seasons.

Spiritual Desert Seasons

In your Christian life experiences, you sometimes come into seasons where your life feels like you are in a desert or a dry place. If you live a diligent Christian life, it is important that you do not let circumstances cause you to misuse these dry or desert seasons. Why do I say this? There are many dry places in the world, where you can encounter water if you dig deep into the ground. Sometimes, you find trees that survive in these dry places because they sense water and send their roots deep into the ground to reach that water.

In your dry or desert seasons, the Lord guides you and satisfies your desires because you do not allow the dryness to deter you from seeking more of Him or His presence. You sense the Holy Spirit, the River of living water, urging you to draw closer to your God. Consequently, the Lord revives your bones and makes you like a watered garden (Isaiah 58:11). You become like a watered garden because you contact the water of life in Jesus Christ. It waters you even in your dry or desert seasons. You may fall seven times in some seasons from calamity but will rise again (Proverbs 24:16).

LESSON: *In your dry or desert seasons, the Lord expects you to put out your roots deep into Him, to contact the water of Life in Him.*

The Bible says in Jeremiah 17:7-8 that you are blessed because you trust in the Lord and make Him your hope. Therefore, you will be as a tree planted by a stream, which sends its roots into a stream. My friend, because you seek God's presence, and you trust and make Him your confidence, even in your seasons of dryness, you will be like that tree and God's presence will feed you with life. You will flourish because His presence will encamp around you like a shield and keep you revived. You will not fear when heat comes. You will remain "green" and will not be anxious in the year of drought, and you will not cease to bear fruit. My friend, I declare these blessings to come on your life.

The eyes of the Lord run to and fro in all the whole earth to show Himself strong on behalf of those whose heart is perfect toward Him (2 Chronicles 16:9). Your diligence in the pursuit of the attributes of your new identity in Christ and yielding to God through obedience activates His powerful presence with you. It quickens something on the inside of you, which makes you crave for more of His presence. You desire His presence because there, you find your fulfillment and joy.

The Psalmist said in Chapter 16 and verse 11, "You make known to me the path of life; in your presence there is fullness of joy; at your right hand are pleasures forevermore." The path of life is the pursuit of righteousness, the fear of the Lord, holiness, and godliness. King David said in Psalms 23:3 that God will lead you in the path of righteousness for His name's sake. In many instances in my own life, I have felt the Lord disabling the fleshly motivations I could have used to do something stupid or unrighteous. This is how I understood Philippians 2:13.

By His Spirit, God motivates you, helping you do what is right in your life issues. Doing what is right implies obedience to His Word, which, as I indicated earlier, activates the presence of both the Son and the Father.

In your seasons of drought, the Lord wants you to grow your roots deeper into Him. He wants you to deepen your understanding of His ways, so that your faith and trust in Him can grow. This is how you would gain a revealed knowledge of God. It stabilizes you in life issues. Jesus said when people do not have roots, they are unable to endure the onslaughts of the world (Matthew 13:21). You are stable in your Christian life because you have grown deep roots into Jesus Christ. You grow in your assurance of faith, knowing that God is with you always.

Your desire and love for righteousness gives you a childlike attitude towards life and God—a poor and contrite spirit, which trembles at God's Word. God loves to abide in people with such spirits and hearts. Remember, God said in Isaiah 57:15b, "I dwell in the high and holy place, and also with him who is of a contrite and lowly spirit, to revive the spirit of the lowly, and to revive the heart of the contrite". Your humble and contrite heart activates the presence of God.

Psalm 140:13 says, "Surely the righteous shall give thanks to your name; the upright shall dwell in your presence". Since your new identity in Christ has righteousness, walk in righteousness and enjoy a growing presence of God with you.

LESSON: *Refuse to chain yourself to the routine of doing so much in life and fail to seek God's presence. Do not build your life on a shaky foundation for your tomorrow's divine inheritance.*

When you lack the presence of God, you become vulnerable to the influence of the world in many critical areas of your life. In Acts Chapter 10, Cornelius, a centurion and a Gentile, acknowledged God's presence with him. The Bible says he feared God with his whole house. Cornelius gave alms generously to people, and prayed to God continually.

In the temple of King Solomon was a table for the bread that represented the presence of God (2 Chronicles 4:19). It was a requirement that they keep bread always on this table. Learn to present yourself as the "table" on which the presence of God will love to abide.

Usually, the knowledge of the presence of God with you promotes the fear of Him. This is what helps you depart from the evil ways of the world. Your knowledge of God's presence with you will motivate obedience to His voice, His Word. When you grow in obedience, it enlarges God's presence and His power in your life. God anointed Jesus Christ with the Holy Spirit and with power. He went about doing good for people and healing all who were oppressed by the devil, because the presence of God was with Him (Act 10:38). Jesus was obedient totally to God His Father.

Learn to depend on God alone. View all the good things that come to you as from Him, even your unexpected life issues. Because you depend on God, He gives you wisdom to know His ways. He is your Shepherd and He supplies all your needs by Christ Jesus. Therefore, you shall not want! The good things that help stabilize your life in Christ come from above, from your Father in Heaven.

LESSON: *One of the best things a Christian can understand is that it is not about how much you do, but how you do all you do. In all your doing, do so with the awareness of God's presence so you would please Him.*

As a person who has an identity in Christ and the calling of God on your life, view the presence of God as the "hottest commodity" you can buy in this very turbulent world. In the book of Exodus, God spoke to and encouraged Moses on how he had found favor in His eyes. He said to Moses in Exodus 33:14, "My presence will go with you, and I will give you rest." To be certain of God's presence, Moses made it clear to God, "If Your presence will not go with me, do not bring us up from here".

Why was God's presence so important to Moses? Moses realized God's presence as the only factor that defined them as different from all other peoples and nations on the face of the earth (Exodus 33:16). Moreover, Moses realized the presence of God as the only assurance of deliverance from any difficulty they could encounter in their journey through cities and nations.

Jesus lived in God's presence and knew God's presence was with Him. In fact, He made it clear to the disciples in John 16:32, "You will be scattered, each to his own home, and will leave Me alone. Yet I Am not alone, for the Father is with Me." The presence of God in the life of Jesus made all the difference in His life and ministry on the earth. He was able to function in the fullness of the power of God's Holy Spirit, and with the highest integrity and self-control. He could have called legions of angels to His defense while the Roman soldiers physically dehumanized Him, but He did not!

LESSON: *If you are a Christian who worries about what people do to you or fail to do for you, you probably do not have enough knowledge of God's presence with you.*

The presence of God with you, and your awareness of His presence, will fortify you against offense, which is so common in this world. Your knowledge of God with you will also keep you from the many corruptible and evil ways in this world. One thing corruption seeks in your life is to diminish God's presence with you, which can happen if you yield to it. When King David sinned against Uriah and his wife Beersheba, his dread was the possibility of losing the presence of God. He cried out to God, "Do not cast me away from Your presence, And do not take Your Holy Spirit from me" (Psalm 51:11).

Room for God's Presence

Learn to make room in your life that invites the presence of God. I want to give you a short list of some of the things you can do to invite God's presence:

1. Engage God in a constant conversation (Ephesians 6:18) with a sincere and humble heart.
2. The Heaven is God's throne and the earth is His footstool but He looks for a house to build for His resting place (Isaiah 66:1). God looks for a place of rest. You have an identity in Christ so you have an advantage to have God's presence with you. Your humility in life, your contrite spirit, and your trembling at His word (obedience) will make you His resting place (Isaiah 66:2).

    Learn to allow the influence of God's Word to define your daily decisions and choices. It will grow humility and create a contrite heart in you. Then you will be a place where God establishes His presence—His place of rest.
3. Grow your conviction for God's Word. It will grow your faith. Strong conviction activates actions in behavior and deeds. The foundation of faith is conviction in God's Word and promises. Therefore, faith

conviction helps your obedience to God in your life issues. Your life will therefore invite the approval and the pleasure of God.

Apostle John wrote, "Let what you heard from the beginning abide in you. If what you heard from the beginning abides in you, then you too will abide in the Son and in the Father" (1 John 2:24).

LESSON: *Your obedience to God's Word is proof that you know Him and His Word has found an abiding place in you.*

One of God's plans for you is to have His fullness in you (Ephesians 3:19). The prerequisite for this is to ground your life in love for God and for people in obedience to His Word (1 John 5:3). Your obedience creates or makes room in you for God's presence. It invites the presence of the Father and Son in your life. Jesus was completely obedient to His Father and He walked in the fullness of God's presence and power.

4. Find and meditate on as many of the promises of God as you can find. Obey the Word of God and make it a part of your life's daily decisions and choices. Apply them in your life situations. This is how you keep God's Word or commandments.

5. Get involved with what God is doing on the earth and learn to reach out to the lost. Align yourself with His love for people.

6. Acknowledge God in all of your ways. Commit all your concerns and cares to Him (Proverbs 3:6)—depend and trust God.

Grow your awareness of the presence of the "Immanuel"—the God with you. True awareness of God's presence will influence your life and lifestyle. It will produce boldness in you to live for Him. It will grow your daily walk of righteousness, holiness, and obedience.

As you learn to obey God's Word, you learn to fear Him and His presence will encamp around you like a shield (Psalm 34:7). More wisdom will enter your heart to help enlarge your revelation knowledge of God's nature (Proverbs 2:1-10) and His requirement for your life. Then your life and lifestyle will show that indeed, you know God. You will gain an inner revelation of God as the One who practices steadfast love, justice, and righteousness in the earth (Jeremiah 9:23-24).

The presence of God in your life provides a covering from the plots of evil men, even the tongue of the wicked (Psalm 31:20). Because of your knowledge of God's presence, you will not subscribe to the hasty lifestyle of the world. The Bible says whoever believes will not be in haste (Isaiah 28:16b). He goes before you and He is your rear guard.

Greater levels of God's presence in your life are contingent. Therefore, orient your life to know and comprehend humility. God says, "Walk humbly before Me in this life" (Micah 6:8). Humility is not like the folding of hands. True humility is an inner orientation that acknowledges the awesomeness of God. Consequently, it influences your inward and outward attitudes in the world and in your interpersonal relationships.

LESSON: *One error you may be tempted to make is to allow life's needs to take precedent over your hunger for more of God's presence with you.*

Importance of God's Presence

God's presence was visible in the life of the shepherd boy David. God's presence with David in his shepherding assignments enabled him to kill a lion and a bear in order to rescue a lamb that they took from the flock. God's presence is a covering and protection for your life.

Apostle Paul knew God's presence was with him. He worshiped Him even in his imprisonment. He turned the prison into a "worship session" and truly, the presence of God broke the shackles off him and the other prisoners (Acts 16:16-26). Paul was convinced of God's presence and he knew His voice. He did not allow fellow believers to dissuade him when the Holy Spirit commanded him to go to Jerusalem (Acts 21:11-14).

The presence of God with you makes you unique among all peoples on the earth. Your spiritual enemies see and know the level of God's presence with you. They back off after they unsuccessfully try you for a season. The devil backed off for a season when he could not get Jesus to sin against God in the wilderness (Luke 4:13).

Hindrance to God's Presence

In all you do in this life, acknowledge God as a holy supreme being, who calls you to holiness (1 Peter 1:16). You are the one who is serious about your salvation. You know and understand the demands of your identity in Christ Jesus. Therefore, you have the ability to identify the things in life that contend against your ability to grow your awareness of God's presence and a desire for more of Him.

The presence of God was the greatest heart's desire of many of the forerunners of our faith. God wants you to seek His presence too. No man could kill (or take the life of) Jesus. He had to lay down His life. He bore the sins of the world and the presence of God turned away from Him (John 10:17-18). Then, He cried, "My God, My God, why have You forsaken Me" (Mark 14:34).

Therefore, fleshly lifestyles, disobedience, wickedness, and a lifestyle of sin and evil turn off the light of God's presence. Check your life for things that hinder the power of God's presence with you. I will present some hindrances to the presence of God. Go down the following list of hindrances and see if you can find any that stand in the way of God's presence growing in your life.

- **Disobedience:** Do you, as a habit, fail to practice God's Word you know in your life issues? It is rebellion! God expects you to learn to define your daily life issues by His Word (2 Peter 1:4).
- **Rebellion:** It is an intentional, consistent rejection of God's Word or command for your selfish inner drive in life issues. Avoid allowing rebellion to become a lifestyle. The Bible says rebellion is as the sin of witchcraft.
- **Wickedness:** It is important to note that you fall into sinful acts sometimes depending on your level of maturity in Christ. However, it is one thing to fall into sin and completely another when you intentionally plan and execute evil deeds.
- **Ignoring knowledge of God:** This is where you knowingly ignore growing your knowledge of God's Word and His ways for your selfish worldly ways and pursuits.
- **Lack of the fear of the Lord:** When lacking an awesome regard for God.
- **Serving God with a fleshly mentality:** Here, you place your faith in money and things of the world, rather than God.
- **Misplaced Dependency:** When your faith rests in the wisdom of men rather than the power of God and His Word. It is a lack of trust in the Lord.
- **Doubting God as a lifestyle:** You may doubt God once a while depending on the level of your maturity. However, when you doubt Him on a continuum, you could loose God's presence because He and His Word are one.

Lacking Knowledge of God's Presence—Some Indicators

Understand the presence of God with you! It means God is with you wherever you are. It does not imply that you pray and invite His presence. Because of your identity in Christ and your willingness to put on the attributes of your new creation, God's presence is uniquely with you. You share His divine nature and He delights to come to you in each of your life issues.

Some of these things may be present in the lives of people who lack the knowledge of God's presence:

- They say and do things and go to places that compromise the Christian lifestyle without the slightest restraint.
- They sustain thoughts that compromise the standards of Christian living without the slightest restraint.
- They trust more in the things of the flesh than the promises and the Word of God.
- They compromise the righteous standards of God by indulging in the same underhanded deeds like those walking in darkness.
- They fear the future as any other person in the world.
- They are controlled by fear and anxiety in their times of trouble.
- They are perplexed and confused in the time of trouble.
- They are filled with hatred, backbiting of others, and fleshly competitiveness as the people of the world.
- They maintain and enjoy being at quarreling and feuding with others without any concern of the spiritual consequences.
- They make right choices and decisions only when other Christians are around, but are contrary to God's ways in the absence of others. This is a double standard Christian lifestyle.

Some Benefits of God's Presence

- God's presence with you will create a path through your daily problems. Its helps you navigate through your daily life problems without unfaithfulness to God.
- God's presence will always lead you in triumph (2 Corinthians 2:14).
- It helps you to live differently in this corrupt world. You learn to separate from the evil ways of the world and therefore, people see and

acknowledge that you are different. They recognize that the way you talk, think, and respond to life issues is different from their method.

- It brings a recognizable difference between you and the rebellious world in the eyes of the powers of darkness (Acts 19:11-15).
- God's presence with you will increase you in wisdom, understanding, knowledge, and the fear of the Lord. It also grows the spirit of counsel and might in all you do.
- The presence of God brings glory and honor. It provides you with strength and gladness (1 Chronicles 16: 27) and fullness of joy (Psalms 16:11).
- The presence of God will go ahead of you. It will part your "Red Seas" and make ways through your challenges.
- It helps you come to a place of rest (Exodus 33:14).
- Fruitfulness and effectiveness will show in your Christian life.
- It helps you overcome the temptation and distractions that cause deviation from what is righteous.

It frustrates the plans of the enemy against your life. He is not able to get you off God so he can do to you what he wants.

Chapter 11

Sustaining the Fire of Identity:
Routine Prayer and Fasting

A strong Christian life starts on the foundation of the born-again experience. The power of the Christian life starts with the baptism of the Holy Spirit. The born-again experience is a dynamic occurrence, authenticated by baptism with the Holy Spirit and Fire. It is the source of the power of your new identity in Christ. After these spiritual experiences happen in your life, it is your responsibility to keep the fire of your new spiritual status always burning.

The people questioned in their hearts if John the Baptist was the Christ. He answered them in Luke 3:16, "I baptize you with water, but He who is mightier than I is coming, the strap of whose sandals I am not worthy to untie. He will baptize you with the Holy Spirit and with fire."

Jesus baptizes you with the Holy Spirit and with Fire. The Holy Spirit in you gains more of your life because you learn to offer your life to God as a holy sacrifice. It brings you to a deeper place in Christ Jesus irrespective of what the world throws at you. In this deeper place, the fire of your new birth grows and keeps burning brighter and brighter. Your capacity enlarges for more of the Holy Spirit and the fire of God as you learn to equip yourself for the "urgent" Christian life.

Apostle Paul received an illumination of the urgency of the times, and he said in 1 Corinthians 7:29-31, "This is what I mean, brothers: the appointed time has grown very short. From now on, let those who have wives live as though they had none, and those who mourn as though they were not mourning, and those who rejoice as though they were not rejoicing, and those who buy as though they had no goods, and those who deal with the world as though they had no dealings with it. For the present form of this world is passing away."

Because of the urgency of the times, do not allow anything to slow you down or quench the fire of who you have become in Christ. Take heed to non-kingdom matters so they do not cause you much headache in your marriage and your life. You have to watch how you involve yourself in your dealings with the world, such as in business matters and personal relationships. Do not let the problems of this life steal the clear mind and conscience you need for prayer. God wants you to be free from anxieties!

God wants you to pray in the Spirit at all times with all prayer and supplication. He wants you to keep alert with all perseverance, and make supplication for the saints (Ephesians 6:18). God wants you to understand that the end of all things is at hand; therefore, learn self-control and be sober-minded for the sake of your prayers (1 Peter 4:7). Why is that necessary? Because your adversary, the devil, prowls around like a roaring lion, seeking someone to devour (1 Peter 5:8b). He comes to steal and kill your passion for Christ.

For the urgency of the times, let prayer and fasting become one of the important "strands of the DNA" of your Christian life. Remember Cornelius! He was not born again but prayed continually to God (Acts 10:1-2). As a born-again believer, learn to pray so more.

Always live in Jesus and learn to pray constantly. Jesus said abide in Him and Him in you because apart from Him you can do nothing (John 15:4-5). Your new life is as a branch attached to Jesus. Therefore, let your life be like a tree that will sink its roots deep into the life (sap) in Jesus. The life of Jesus is your light in this life. Your life embedded in Jesus brings His light to you, which is the Word of life. You abide in Jesus and the Father because you keep the Word of life.

Let much prayer bring you deeper into Christ. You know you cannot live happily in the same house with someone without engaging that person in frequent conversation. If you believe Jesus is in you, then you cannot but engage Him in a constant conversation—prayer!

The Bible commands you to not quench the Spirit (1 Thessalonians 5:19). Because you learn to pray constantly, the Holy Spirit will help keep the fires of your new identity burning. It keeps you always dynamic, sincere, humble, and faithful to the Lord. Unfaithfulness diminishes your ability to walk in the fire of your Holy Spirit baptism. Your faithfulness, through a life of obedience to God's Word activates the presence of both God and Jesus. This is so because:

- In obedience, you define your life issues by the Word of God. It influences the things you choose to do and the decisions and choices you make in this life. This lifestyle affirms you believe in Jesus Christ and you regard Him as your Lord.

- Your obedience to God's Word helps you escape corruption, which orients you to participate in the divine nature of God. You become a vessel in which God delights to dwell.

Why Pray Constantly?

Your ability to walk in the power of your identity in Jesus Christ requires your obedience to God's Word and your constant prayer life. It grows and elevates you to a higher place in Christ because you learn the discipline of constant prayer, routine fasting, and obedience to His word you know. I will give you a few reasons why you have to learn to pray constantly:

- You pray because of your born-again status. Your constant prayer to God is a sign of your dependence on Him.
- God has made you an ambassador for Christ. An ambassador is required to commune with the headquarters to ask for updates of policies. The ambassador would ask for things needed to help to function effectively in the country of assignment. The Holy Spirit makes known (to your spirit) the ways of the Lord because you always come to the throne of grace in prayer.
- You have to pray because Jesus commands you to do so. In Luke 18:1-3, Jesus explained a parable regarding a judge and a widow that teaches on the importance of praying always and not lose heart.
- Again, He said in Matthew 26:41 to watch and pray that you may not enter into temptation. Prayer was the custom of Jesus in His life on the earth. It was His custom to withdraw Himself to the mountain to pray. The particular ways and style of Jesus prayers to His Father in His over-night prayers are unknown. However, His prayer to the Father in John Chapter 17 provides clues.
- Prayer edifies your spirit to help you reign over your weak flesh. When you pray in your native language and with the language of the Holy Spirit, you build yourself up in your faith (Jude 1:20). If you pray constantly and in the Spirit, the Holy Spirit can lead your prayers into areas of your tomorrow's possible problems and difficulties.

Jesus told Apostle Peter in Luke 22:31-32, "Simon, Simon, behold, Satan hath desired to have you, that he may sift you as wheat: But I have prayed for thee, that thy faith fail not: and when thou art converted, strengthen thy brethren." Jesus prayed for Peter ahead of his problem.

Prayer must accompany any period of fasting. Constant fasting without prayer and obedience to the One in whose name you fast means nothing in the spiritual realm. When you submit to God and honor Him in your daily life issues, it activates His presence with you to a much greater level than the ordinary Christian who ignores the demands of his/her new identity in Christ.

In addition to gaining an intellectual knowledge of God through His Word, you are required to live in obedience to the Word that you know. God commands you to find grace to help you serve Him with reverence and godly fear (Hebrews 12:28). Normally, you will obey the one you reverence! If you reverence God, you must learn to obey Him.

What is Fasting and Why Fast?

Fasting is to go without food for a time or period for spiritual purposes. Your goal is to open yourself to God to meet a need in your life. The specified timeframe of the fast depends on what the Holy Spirit is leading you. Normally, fasting is to go without food and water during this period. You have to be on your guard when you want to fast because the flesh could convince you it is dangerous to fast without water. Your fasting is not fleshly but spiritual. If the Spirit of God is leading you to fast, He will provide you with the grace to endure.

Fasting is an integral part of the Christian life and a common lifestyle among God's people. In Matthew 4:1-2, the Holy Spirit led Jesus into the wilderness to go through temptation by the devil. While He was there, He fasted forty days and nights without food and water. In Acts 9:17, the Apostle Paul, then Saul, went for three days without food and water after his transforming encounter with Jesus. In Acts 13:2 while the disciples were worshiping the Lord with fasting, the Holy Spirit told them to separate Barnabas and Saul for His assignment.

Fasting affects your attitude in life and your approach to God. Fasting helps you fulfill Micah 6:8 (KJV), "He hath shewed thee, O man, what is good; and what doth the LORD require of thee, but to do justly, and to love mercy, and to walk humbly with thy God?" If you find your attitudes become aggressive during your time of fasting, you may have started your fast with a wrong cause.

LESSON: *Fasting breaks and humbles you before God. Consequently, it imposes on you a humble attitude towards life and people.*

Psalms 51:17(KJV) says, "The sacrifices of God are a broken spirit: a broken and a contrite heart, O God, thou wilt not despise." Humility in life and before God is a very important Christian experience that you need to learn to pursue as a lifestyle.

One of the lifestyles that activate God's presence is a sincere and constant prayer life. Usually, prayer accompanies fasting because fasting without prayer is no fasting at all! On the other hand, you do not pray only when fasting. Prayer is the lifeblood that runs through the veins of your Christian life. Learn to set yourself up to fast at certain days as a lifestyle. Nevertheless, you have to pray constantly! All who are in Christ are required to pray to avoid temptation.

Learn to pray and fast routinely because of your status in Christ and your baptism in the Holy Spirit. I cannot over emphasize the importance of making prayer and fasting, a part of your Christian lifestyle. John the Baptist said Jesus would baptize not only with the Holy Spirit but also with fire. To ignore this lifestyle of prayer and fasting is to deny yourself the ability to walk in the power of your identity in Christ Jesus. You could slump to a mundane Christian lifestyle and consequently quench the fire of the Holy Spirit in your life.

According to Jesus, the journey to life in Heaven requires passage through a narrow and difficult gate (Matthew 7:14). You confront many life challenges. The chaos of lawlessness in the world presents opportunities to live unfaithful to God. The ability to endure through the chaos to the end will earn you the glory of Christ. Jesus is telling His people to pray always and to not faint or grow weak (Luke 18:1). Again, He wants you to stay awake at all times, praying that you may have strength to escape all the things that are going to take place, and to stand before the Son of Man (Luke 21:36).

It is God's desire that His presence be all over your life. For His presence to abide with you in an increasing measure, there are some things you have to learn about the kind of lifestyle you are to live to protect you from the influence of the chaos of lawlessness in the world. In His love for you, God has given grace to you live a life of fasting and prayer. It helps you endure anything the world and your flesh will attempt to do to tear you down from your secure place in Christ.

There are some important pursuits or lifestyle I refer to as "pillars". You have to learn to build them into your faith life. These pillars will produce stability in your life, irrespective of the changes and moral challenges in this world. These pillars will assist you in maintaining the fire of your identity in Christ Jesus.

If you are one of the unashamed, who seeks a closer walk with Jesus, you may have understood that the closer walk with Christ comes with many difficulties and challenges. Even then, these seven pillars will anchor your soul to the Solid Rock, Jesus, and help maintain your balance no matter how the world tilts by evil morality, selfish motivations, and spiritual decadence. Among many others, I will list the following seven "pillars":

1. Keep the purity of your new self through a life of righteousness.
2. Mature in holiness through a life motivated by the fear of the Lord.
3. Learn to establish and be rooted in the foundation of love for God and for people to help activate the fullness of God in you life.
4. Keep the fires of the Spirit of your baptism always burning through a life of prayer, fasting, and obedience to the Word of God
5. Humble yourself in your approach to life before God and in your interpersonal issues. Grow the "fasted-life".
6. Allow God's Word to define your live convictions, choices, and decisions. It will develop strong and deep roots into your Savior, Jesus Christ, which will strengthen your life of faith.
7. Live a Holy Spirit-motivated life. Live and walk by Him to help you understand and hear God, who is Spirit. This is how you keep your life out of condemnation.

The Holy Spirit helps you build and live these seven pillars. Live by the motivations He gives you and give Him the liberty to lead you daily. Without Him, you would have difficulties in your Christian experiences and journey to the Kingdom.

LESSON: *A Holy Spirit-led life always promotes humility on the outward but on the inward abides the Lion of Judah.*

A life overshadowed by pride, arrogance, and self, indicates interference from other spirits other than the Holy Spirit. The seven pillars listed above add stability to your outward and inward Christian experiences. However, it requires a daily fight to maintain this lifestyle. Therefore, learn to depend on the strength of the Holy Spirit to help you maintain a lifestyle of fasting, prayer, supplication, and the study of God's Word.

As you grow in the knowledge of God's Word, you will increasingly grow in truth and love. The Holy Spirit is the Spirit of Truth. If you live in truth,

He keeps you spiritually covered. Love will enhance your walk in the fear of the Lord. God's goal for you is your conformation into the image of His son, Jesus Christ, who is True and Faithful.

LESSON: *In truth and sincerity, you learn to submit to the "Laws and Rulings" of the "Supreme Court" of God's justice. You do not insist on your own laws and ways when they are against God's Word and His ways.*

The Fasted Lifestyle

In addition to prayer and fasting without food, God looks for a "fasted lifestyle". What do I refer to as a fasted lifestyle? God said to the children of Israel in Isaiah 58:6-7, "Is not this the fast that I choose?" What is the fast that the Lord chooses? It is a lifestyle that "smells" in His nostrils as a fast. These are the following:

1. God wants you to put off wickedness. Wickedness is to know the will of God in life and refuse to practice what He desires.
2. He wants you to undo the heavy burdens. This does not only happen physically, but you could place heavy burdens on people by your attitudes and selfish expectations in your heart. The consequence of failure is offense.
3. He wants you to let the oppressed go free. You may say, "I do not oppress anyone." You see, oppressing someone may not necessarily be physical. When you hold people in your heart due to offense or other disagreements, you oppress them.
4. To break every yoke you place on other people.
5. To share your bread with the hungry, if you have the means to do so.
6. Bring the homeless and poor into your house. This is a very difficult thing to do in regards to this age of wickedness. Nevertheless, the Holy Spirit leads you to do this.
7. To clothe and cover the naked when you see them. You have to learn to share your many clothes with the disadvantaged. There are certain people whose closets look like a clothing store.
8. Not to lift up yourself above your own people—be unapproachable.

The above list is what I call the "the fasted lifestyle". In the eyes of the Lord, this is just a life of fasting. God also told the children of Israel that He had shown them what was good— to do justly, love mercy, and to walk humbly with God in this life (Micah 6:8). You see, you learn to relate to people in a way that is righteous and with integrity, irrespective of who they are.

The fasted lifestyle and righteousness in your relationships makes your fast a very powerful exercise to draw God's attention and response. You cannot have your own way, walking in rebellion or disobedience, and think you can use God as a slot machine by fasting. If you are living in disobedience and rebellion then genuine repentance must precede the fast. God seeks humility from people who serve Him.

The Bible says in Psalms 24:3-6, "Who may ascend the hill of the LORD? Or who may stand in His holy place? He who has clean hands and a pure heart, Who has not lift up his soul to an idol, Nor swore deceitfully. He shall receive blessing from the LORD, And righteousness from the God of his salvation. This is Jacob, the generation of those who seek Him, Who seek Your face." Therefore, you do not only have to learn to fast but also learn to live a life pleasing to the Lord.

Jesus, a Man of Prayer and Fasting

Apostle Paul said some of the things he went through in his Christian life were hunger, thirst, and fasting (2 Corinthians 11:27). At the outskirts of Samaria, the disciples of Jesus urged Him to eat some food. He said to them, "I have food to eat which you do not know" (John 4:32). When Jesus expects to minister to people, He usually would not eat until His ministry was over.

In Mark 9:28-29, the disciples struggled but were unable to cast out an evil spirit from a boy. When Jesus came home, they asked Him why they could not drive out the evil spirit. Jesus told them, "This kind can come out only by prayer and fasting." Does it mean whenever you encounter such a situation, you have to go fast before you can cast out the evil spirit? The answer is *No!*

On the other hand, learn both the fasted lifestyle and scheduled times of fasting as part of your Christian life. Since fasting helps humble you before God, His presence with you will do His work through you. The disciples could not drive out the evil spirit because until then, they had not received the baptism of the power of the Holy Spirit. Moreover, they were not broken or converted yet.

LESSON: *Brokenness is a place you come to in your Christian life where you are not concerned about self-preservation or self-aggrandizement. You also have* *no fear of what people will think or say about your unbendable love for and trust in Jesus. You do not care what people do or fail to do for you.*

Kinds of Fasting

1. Simple fasting

In a simple fast, you take no food for a specified period. At the end of each day you break your fast with water first and then solid food afterwards. If you intend to go on with this fast beyond one day, all eating must stop before midnight each day. Therefore, you can undertake this kind of fast for any number of days as the Holy Spirit leads.

Each day, the fast begins from midnight the previous day and ends at any time within the 24-hour day—noon, 3 PM, or 6 PM, as the Holy Spirit leads. There is an example of this fast recorded in Judges 20:26, "And all the sons of Israel, and all the people, went up and came into the house of God, and wept, and sat there before Jehovah and fasted that day until evening, and offered burnt offerings and peace offerings before Jehovah."

2. Vegetable fast

This is similar to a simple fast except the food for breaking your fast is purely vegetables. In fact, it is not a vegetable fast if you do this for only one day. It has to go beyond one day to qualify as a vegetable fast. As with the simple fast, the time to start and time to end this fast depends on the individual. Know what the Holy Spirit is leading you to do.

3. Absolute (or Dry) fast

This is similar to Jesus' fast. Moses, Elijah, and Esther each fasted in this way. They went for days without food and water. In an absolute fast, you start like any of the other kind of fast. You end this fast at 6:00 PM or midnight on the last day. The last day could be one, three, seven, or any number of days the Holy Spirit is leading you. You have to hear exactly what the Holy Spirit is saying to help you avoid giving opportunity to the devil to hurt you.

There is also a one day absolute fast. In this fast, you start as any other fast. However, you do not break your fast until the next day. It is from midnight the first day to midnight the next day. If you drink water during this fast, it ceases to be absolute.

4. Moderation—Water Fast

If you are not able to go through with absolute fast of no food and water (dry), you can drink water at regular intervals. You can set yourself up to sip water at three-hour intervals throughout the whole time of your fast. In fact, this changes the absolute or any other fast to water fasting.

5. Extended Fast

At the leading of the Holy Spirit, you can embark on an extended fast. Jesus fasted 40 days and nights led by the Holy Spirit (Matthew 4:1-2). Moses went through a 40-day fast when he went up to meet God on the mount of Sinai. Elijah also went for 40 days without food. I will not encourage anyone to attempt this kind of fast unless you are truly, truly directed by the Holy Spirit. Otherwise, do not attempt the extended absolute fast beyond three days.

For any of the above kinds of fasting, you can extend it to any number of days. If it is not absolute, you break the fast at the end of each day. As I indicated, your fast is Holy Spirit directed! Before I started my evangelistic missions to Africa, I went through 40 days of a simple fast.

Some Instructions for Fasting

1. Establishing a Cause for Fasting

Before you embark on a fast as a Christian, it is important that you establish a cause or a reason. You cannot fast just because it is a "cool" spiritual thing to do. First, establish a cause— the reason why you have to fast. Usually, in the sincerity of your heart, the Holy Spirit will prompt you to fast, the kind of fast to embark on, and the number of days to fast. These instructions come to you at the same time. Do not allow your flesh cause you to modify what the Holy Spirit instructs you to do.

- **No Pride**

The fact that you fast is not a reason for pride. The Pharisees prided themselves because they fasted. A Pharisee prayed in Luke 18:12, "I fast twice a week; I give tithes of all that I get".

- **Avoid Temptation to Sin**

Oftentimes, it is easy to handle a day of fasting. On the other hand, when you fast more than a day or two, the body usually will cry for food. Learn to handle the pain of hunger correctly because if you fail to do so, people's attitudes and bad behavior could aggravate you to sin.

After He fasted for forty days and forty nights, Jesus became physically exhausted and hungry. At this point of hunger, the tempter came to tempt Him. He said to Jesus, "If you are the Son of God, command that these stones be made bread (Matthew 4:2-3).

Satan tried to tempt Jesus to exhibit self-will and fleshly desires through obedience to his command. These are lessons to help you overcome in your times of fasting. Always remember, your fasting is to God and for your own benefit. You do not fast to show anyone your spirituality.

God Responds to Fasting

Elijah spoke to King Ahab, informing him of what God intended to do in his life in response to his evil ways. The Bible says that when Ahab heard those words, he rent his clothes, put sackcloth upon his flesh, and fasted and lay in sackcloth. His brokenness and humility activated God's attention. God said to the Prophet Elijah, "Have you seen how Ahab has humbled himself before Me? Because he has humbled himself before Me, I will not bring the evil in his days; but in his son's days I will bring the evil upon his house" (1 Kings 21:27- 29).

God said in 2 Chronicles 7:14, "If My people who are called by My name humble themselves, and pray and seek My face, and turn from their wicked ways, then I will hear from heaven, and will forgive their sin and heal their land."

It is important to note the key phrases in this last passage.

- If My people who are called by My name
- Humble themselves and pray and seek My face

- Turn from their wicked ways
- I will hear from Heaven

If you fast with a sincere and humble heart, God will respond because of the humbling of your heart. It is not necessarily the fasting but the humbling of your heart that God responds. Learn to turn from evil ways. Therefore, learn to establish routine times for fasting and prayer to help you always humble your heart before God. Humility before God will enhance your Christian maturity because a humble heart activates God's presence with you.

Chapter 12
Identity and Situational Faith

Now faith is the assurance of things hoped for, the conviction of things not seen—Hebrews 11:1.

Situational faith is what you do with the Word and promises of God in response to your urgent or current life situation or need. Your responses to your life situation in the face of life difficulties define whether you have strong or weak faith. I refer to this faith as "identity-motivated faith" because you are required to respond to your life situation or need with confidence and belief in God's Word. You have become a part of God's household and His possession due to your identity in Christ. God's mode of operation is faith and He wants you to live, walk, and respond to life situations and issues by faith.

The Word of God is powerful, living, and very active. It is sharper than any two-edged sword, piercing to the division of soul and of spirit, of joints and of marrow, and can discern the thoughts and intentions of a man's heart (Hebrews 4:12).

Call to Faith

Your identity in Christ brings you into a divine relationship with God. This relationship places a demand on you to know Him and His ways. God wants you to learn to walk and to live in truth and by His Spirit. The God who created your identity in Christ is Spirit and He desires all who come to Him to do so with the knowledge that He exists and He rewards those who seek Him diligently (Hebrews 11:6). The reward from God can revolutionize your entire life, either spiritually or in the natural.

God is invisible and no one has seen or can see Him. Therefore, to seek or trust Him in your life situations requires an act of faith. God is the King of ages, immortal, invisible, the only true God, who deserves honor and glory forever and ever, Amen (1 Timothy 1:17). He is not subject to time because

He lives in the past, the present, and the future all at the same time. He is the God of yesterday, today, and forever. He responds to all who put their trust in Him for their moment-by-moment life needs.

God wants you to learn to trust Him for your entire life needs, even your seasons of confusion and anxieties. By faith, you reverence God and serve Him with godly fear and He gives you the confidence and the wisdom to know that He will come through for you in your pressing times of need. Convince yourself that indeed, God is not far from you.

Even though you do not see God, convince yourself that He cares about your good times and your difficult times. This places a demand on you to live humbly before Him and in faith. He is aware of all that goes on in His entire universe, including your life. God knows the sincerity of your faith and your trust in Him. He knows all you need in life but He supplies them in seasons and in His own times. You can therefore depend on Him in trust.

Living and walking by faith demonstrates your submission to God's will and your dependency on Him. In Mark 9:23, He says, "All things are possible for the one who believes." If you entrust God with your life situations as Jesus did, you will come to know His faithfulness.

When you are born again, you come into a relationship with God on a high spiritual level than other people because He invests the Holy Spirit in you. He gives you grace and His precious promises (His Word) to help you start a spiritual relationship with Him. By His grace, you grow in your ability to know Him and His ways. Therefore, God's expectation is that when your life hits some "hard" places, you will respond by faith to His pleasure. God expects you to draw from your knowledge of Him and His promises to help you respond to life situations by faith.

The identity-motivated situational faith is the God-kind of faith. This is faith based on your conviction of God's faithfulness and ability to fulfill His promise in your life after the Holy Spirit had dropped a hope in your heart for a need. You have a cloud of witnesses who tell about the faithfulness of God but you have to come to that knowledge yourself. God loves you and cares about everything in your life. You have to believe that God is true to every iota of His Word or promises to you. He cannot be God if He fails to fulfill His Word.

This nature of God gives you the confidence to exercise your faith for your life situations. You can trust God with your life's hopes and situations, knowing that He cannot lie! He is the only One in the universe whose Word shall stand forever. His Word is as the rain and the snow, which comes down from heaven and does not return to heaven, but waters the earth, making it bring forth and sprout, giving seed to the one who sows and bread to the one who eats. Likewise, God's Word, which goes out of His mouth, will not return to Him void, but shall accomplish what He pleases, and it shall certainly do what He sends it to do (Isaiah 55:10-11).

Heaven will classify you as having weak or strong faith depending on whether or not you have an unwavering trust in God's ability to fulfill His Word in your time of need. The Bible says in 1 John 1:1, "In the beginning was the Word, and the Word was with God, and the Word was God". Acknowledging God's Word as true will activate a strong conviction in your heart to believe Him to fulfill your hopes. Conviction will move you to act as though you have the things you hope from God.

In exercising your faith, you may not necessarily have tangible evidence of what you hope for and events around you may seem dismal. However, you are undaunted by what your natural eyes see because you look at your hope with your eyes of faith. In situational faith, you declare and follow through with strong convictions of the things you hope for in your current life situation.

In faith, you have to see your hope with your spiritual eyes because, "We look not to the things that are seen but to the things that are unseen" (2 Corinthians 4:18). If you see what you hope for with your spiritual eyes, and then speak it out or live as though you have it, your faith will please God. If you wait to see a thing with your natural eyes before applying faith, it ceases to be faith, because faith depends on hope you do not see.

The Dynamics of Situational Faith

Situational faith begins with a desire the Holy Spirit activates in your heart. When the Holy Spirit activates a desire in your heart, you do not see it, so you hope for it. However, if you pursue the desire with a strong conviction of faith, it will happen for you.

Understand the God you serve. He operates in the now! He is the Alpha and Omega and He is the same yesterday, today, and forever. He speaks and it manifests immediately because there is no time with Him. Though He has seasons in relations with man, He operates in the now. For God, a thousand years is today, now, in His eyes. Since all your needs are not beyond a thousand years, His promises are applicable to you in His today. However, since God is a good Father, He does not load all your needs on you at one time. At specific seasons in your life, the Holy Spirit activates a desire in your heart applicable to your life in the now.

Understand that for God, your yesterday, your today, and your future needs are all in His now. If the Holy Spirit activates a desire in your heart, then the fulfillment is in God's now. The level of your faith conviction will determine the interval before the tangible manifestation of the need. Your conviction of faith pulls your need from the unseen into the seen.

Therefore, understand the godly nature of your new identity in Christ and let it help you walk with God in His now as a person of strong faith. Do not walk with God with uncertainty, in your past or in your future. Learn to live in God's now. Jesus said do not be anxious about tomorrow, for tomorrow will be anxious for itself. He said sufficient for the day is its own trouble (Matthew 6:34).

Grow your level of faith convictions for your now needs. Convince yourself that the Word of God is true and backed by His integrity. The Word of God is the foundation on which your faith thrives. His Word is not powerful only when your life situations seem to move along smoothly. It is powerful even in the midst of your troubles. Your conviction of God's Word to fulfill what you hope for (your desire) is the foundation of your strong faith. It makes your faith deep and powerful. If you are convinced of God's Word, you defy carelessness sneaking in to motivate you to accept voices of doubt, either internally or externally.

Though you do not see God with your natural eyes, you see His Word. God is His Word! Suppose the CEO of your company sends out a memo to all employees calling on them to perform an urgent action. In this situation, no employee will doubt the memo. No one will demand to see the CEO before performing the action required. They will all carry out the demand of the memo immediately without delay or question.

You trust your bank to keep your money and you have no doubt of their ability to do so. You do not go to the bank to seek proof of their ability to keep your money before you open an account with them. You probably know they have been around for a while. Therefore, you trust to do business with them. Your God has been around before all things came into being. You can trust Him with your every life situation, problems, and needs, even your life. Your God is eternal and abides in eternity. He lives in the now! The Bible says God is in the high and lofty place. To God, yesterday, today, and your future are all in the now.

LESSON: *Your inability to trust God in your life situations, even in your overwhelming "crushing" needs, makes Him a cheap God. It places God on the same level as man, who cannot always be trusted.*

Faith—In His Likeness

I said in chapter two that God has restored to you His DNA because of your born-again status. You now have a spiritual identity in Jesus. He has given you a measure of faith to help you function as your Father. He takes delight in you because you function like Him in your life. With the godly nature of your new self (identity), God wants you to believe in Him and His Word, to help you pursue your hopes with strong conviction of faith.

By faith, He spoke, and Lazarus, who was dead four days, came out of the tomb back to life. In your life situation when a need confronts you, do not let your heart look for your hope as a future occurrence. See what you hope for as in the now because your God works in the now. Then, based on God's Word of promise, declare that your need come now.

However, it does not imply that you have to go around hoping and declaring for everything. As I indicated earlier, the Holy Spirit activates a desire in your heart. If you pursue these desires by a strong conviction of faith, God will fulfill them. Do not let doubt defeat your opportunity to see miracles happen in your life.

Establishing the Foundation for Your Faith

For your faith to be effective and sustainable, establish a foundation for your faith to stand on. Verify the convictions that motivate your heart to believe God for the things of your hope. Ensure it is not a desire to satisfy the flesh. Your faith foundation is the Word of God. Below I will touch on two kinds of foundation for faith.

• Fleshly Foundation for Faith

A fleshly foundation of faith draws its confidence from the world's ways and beliefs, worldly worth, strength, wealth, knowledge of research findings, and man's ideas. God said through the prophet Jeremiah that the wise man should not glory or boast in his wisdom. The mighty man should not glory in his might and the rich man in his riches. Rather, the one who glories or boasts, should glory in his/her understanding and knowledge of God, that He is the Lord who practices steadfast love, justice, and righteousness in the earth. This is what earns God's delight (Jeremiah 9:23-24).

People do many phenomenal things in life because they draw their inspiration and strength from their God-given natural abilities. Unfortunately, many of them have no knowledge of this truth in Jeremiah Chapter 9. They fail to ask why them and not others. Even though the foundation of their faith accomplishes some phenomenal things in life, corruption could easily step in their lives because of the ways and means by which they glory in their victories.

• Godly Foundation for Faith

The godly foundation says, "I can do all things through Christ who strengthens me" (Philippians 4:13). Therefore, this faith has its foundation built on the power and ability of God and on His promises. Learn to regard God as your refuge and your present help in your every day's needs or troubles. Build your foundation on His Word.

God has been the source of your various victories in your past, which has brought you to where you are today. These victories, irrespective of size, give you the confidence that God is able to help you in your current life situation. Consequently, let these become the foundation for your faith conviction and do not waver.

After you establish a foundation for your faith, take steps towards your convictions, like a bulldog. You do not make any room for doubt to sneak into your heart. Apostle Paul wrote about the convictions that gave Abraham the willingness to proceed with God's command to sacrifice Isaac. In Hebrews 11:19, Abraham concluded that God was able to resurrect Isaac, even from the dead.

Do not declare your conviction of faith based on the status of your situation because some situations can "mute" or inject fear in your heart. Neither should you declare your faith based on your significance or insignificance in this world. Rather, learn to declare your faith convictions from your hope and knowledge of God's ability.

David's Example: David said to Goliath, "You come to me with a sword and with a spear and with a javelin, but I come to you in the name of the Lord of hosts, the God of the armies of Israel, whom you have defied." David laid his faith foundation on the power and ability of the name of the Lord of Hosts.

Declaring Faith, based on Your Foundation

Because David established the foundation of his faith, he said to the giant, "The Lord will deliver you into my hand, and I will strike you down and cut off your head. And I will give the dead bodies of the host of the Philistines this day to the birds of the air and to the wild beasts of the earth, that all the earth may know that there is a God in Israel" (1 Samuel 17:46). Then in 1 Samuel 17:47b, David repeated the basis of his faith, "For the battle is the Lord's, and He will give you into our hand".

What is the situation in your life that seems to defy God's Word and promises to you? Every knee will bow to Jesus, the Word of God, and every tongue will confess that your God is the only God Almighty! Like David, today, in prayer, you can say to your mountains of problems, challenges, and assignments of the devil, "Who are you that you should defy the Word and promises of God to me? You come against me with your devices and weapons, but I take authority over you in the name of the exalted king, Jesus Christ" (2 Corinthians 10:3-5). When all was set, David drew near to Goliath and he drew near to David. When Goliath saw David, he disdained him because David was but a youth, ruddy and handsome.

LESSON: *Whenever you are intoxicated with your strong faith in God's ability in your time of need, your enemies see beauty in your face. It "freezes" them for the angel of the Lord to get a good shot at their advance.*

LESSON: *Do not be intimidated by the size of your problem or the words of discouragement from people. Set your heart and mind fully on the One who can create from nothing.*

LESSON: *Realize that David declared what God would do for him before he engaged Goliath in the battle.*

Avoid Substitution

God has granted to humanity the opportunity to advance in Christ Jesus. Today, you have the opportunity to abide in Christ and to grow in the revealed knowledge of God's ability to provide and to protect. You can gain knowledge of God's Kingdom, even the secrets of the Kingdom. You also have the ability to know what the world has to say about life issues. If you fail to build your beliefs in God's ability, you could default to all the world has to offer in your time of need, which is not what you need as a Christian.

LESSON: *If you become full of faith based on the words of man, you could unfortunately judge God's ability by what the world says. This is what I refer to as "substitution-substituting faith" in God's Word with the voices in the world.*

When you judge God by the world's rules and beliefs, you limit Him from doing miracles in your life. You lose the opportunity to see the impossibilities become possible. Consequently, your impossibilities become impossible indeed! For this reason, examine what motivations propel your faith in your time of need.

Lifting Self above God's Will

Faith pleases God because it produces actions that tell God you believe and trust in Him alone. Faith is like yielding control to the God you do not see but believe in! Note that whenever you draw your confidence from God's Word in your times of challenges and needs, it is equivalent to humility and obedience to Him. It is humbling your heart under the power of His Word.

God commanded King Saul in 1 Samuel 15:3, "Now go and strike Amalek and devote to destruction all that they have. Do not spare them." This was God's judgment of Amalek. This was God's direct command to King Saul through the Prophet Samuel. Unfortunately, King Saul did God's command in his own way to please and promote self. Today, you and I have God's written commands and His instructions through the Holy Spirit in life issues.

You can trust and believe God's Word and His commands in your pressing times. If not, you would do things that satisfy or promote self. You should always remember that you and I no longer belong to ourselves but to God.

Self-promotion is one of the challenges man contends against daily. Man oftentimes wants people to know what he has done or can do. Deny the enemy's enticement to cause you to take glory for what you do or can do. In fact, if you acknowledge and ascribe glory to God for what you do or can do, you will leave no room for the enemy to trick your heart to exalt self.

King Saul is a typical example of a believer who lifts up self above God's Word. King Saul sought to gain great honor by carrying out God's command in his own ways. Jesus humbled Himself by doing everything exactly as God commanded Him. King Saul spared the king of Amalek and their fatty cattle under the pretence that he was going to sacrifice to the God who commanded him to destroy all. What an honor it brought to him, to parade the king of a nation he had conquered.

LESSON: *Self-aggrandizement should never become a part of the life of the Christian redeemed by the blood of Jesus Christ. Never boast of your strong faith because you are who you are due to God's grace.*

In the pursuit of his own agenda, with lack of faith in God who sent him, King Saul could not trust God's command to do His will. God always appoints people to places of authority and He places His anointing on them for His own specific purposes. You and I will do well to understand the reason for our place or position of authority and the anointing on our lives. You have to ask yourself, "Why me and not another?"

Know that your life has a link to Jesus as a branch on a vine because of your new identity in Him. Everything you do and have is from the vine, and without Him, you can do nothing for your Christian victories and successes (John 15:5)! Trust Him in every one of your life situations so the glory of your victory will go to Him alone and not to you. Humility before God and under His mighty hand is always an attribute of spiritual maturity. Jesus said if you take on and learn of His yoke of meekness and lowliness in heart, you will find rest for your soul (Matthew 11:29-30).

On another occasion, King Saul hurried himself to offer burnt offerings and peace offerings because Samuel, who was to offer these sacrifices, delayed. This was a responsibility for the priest and prophet alone. Out of fear of life circumstances, King Saul hurried to do what the law did not permit him. He feared the Philistines could come down against him at Gilgal while Samuel delayed (1 Samuel 13:8-12). Saul's action was a complete contrast to Jehoshaphat, who depended on the Lord to rescue him.

LESSON: *Do not allow fear and anxiety to motivate you to lose patience and to hurry yourself into doing things you think will bring you peace and victory in your time of need. Trust God and do only what the Holy Spirit is telling you to do. Then your victory will spring forth like the sun.*

Assurance of Hope

God knows everything and about everyone on this planet Earth. He knows every one of your daily needs, even what you will need ten years from now. He said to the prophet Jeremiah, "Before I formed you in the womb I knew you, and before you were born I consecrated you; I appointed you a prophet to the nations" (Jeremiah 1:5).

In the right season of your life, when the Holy Spirit activates a desire or a hope in your heart, do not doubt the possibility of its fulfillment. Your faith becomes your assurance for the fulfillment of the hope or desire that dropped in your heart, though you do not see. This is where conviction becomes very important. You have to speak the fulfillment of your desire or hope with a strong faith conviction as though you already have what you desire.

Speak of your hope or desire as though you have it even when you do not see it in your hands. After you receive a desire in the heart, and your faith, assurance, and conviction are in place, what you do from then on is critical. It is good to have a scripture passage as an anchor for your faith.

To hope for a thing is to have anticipation for something good. You look forward for something good to happen for you. The Bible says hope that is seen ceases to be hope because you cannot hope for what you see (Romans 8:24). In hope, you form a mental picture of what you desire in your spiritual eyes. Your strong conviction propels you to view it as happening for you. God wants to bestow favor and honor on your life and will not withhold any good thing from you if you diligently walk with Him by faith.

LESSON: *Do not define God's ability to fulfill your hope by the magnitude of your need. Define your life need by God's overwhelming power and ability. He has power to call into existence what is not as though it had been.*

Your life situation does not control what God can do for you. Let God's overwhelming power define your situation or need, irrespective of how massive it is. Therefore, do not let your life situation convince you to develop negative hope. In your strong assurance of hope, you will find God as your partner in your life issues. You will come to know that He cares about you more than you have ever known. He is a Dad who is closer to you in every hopeful and hopeless situation. At all cost, do not allow negative hope to blindside you from God- ordained opportunities in life.

In your strong assurance of hope in God's ability and your trust in Him, convince yourself that there is nothing that can do you harm if He has not permitted it. Therefore, if you get a headache, do not prophesy that something bad is happening to you.

Negative hope gives the devil the legal ground to work against you. Your positive assurance of hope and declarations gives God the legal ground to work for you. You do not want to give the devil opportunity to take advantage over your life situation. No matter how bleak your life situation, maintain your positive hope and speak life into your circumstance. As you read in Jeremiah, God wants you to see your life situation and circumstances with the eyes of faith. God wants you to declare a thing and He will hasten to perform it.

Therefore, learn to overcome doubt. Everything about your God is certain and "now". With Him, all things are possible and all things will be possible for you if you refuse to doubt. This is one of the pathways to functioning in the power of your identity in Christ.

Understand that before your mother conceived you in her womb, God already saw your situations coming. He already has solutions to deal with your life situations before your conception in your mother's womb. However, He needs your cooperation and your strong assurance of faith that He is able to help you.

Chapter 13
Passionate (Crazy) Faith

Crazy faith is the kind of faith you need when life-pressing issues come upon you suddenly and you need an urgent solution. In such situations, your heart cries for God's mercy and miraculous interventions to fulfill your need. In crazy faith, your need takes hold of your heart and mind as though you are intoxicated with God's ability to fulfill what you need. It is a strong passionate belief in God's ability to help. It is a correct response or cooperation with the motivations the Holy Spirit brings to you. Consequently, you quickly cooperate with Him to help you receive His directions for your victory.

While walking in crazy faith, you see God as the only source your life depends on, without whom your life would be bankrupt. Consequently, you mentally cut off all other deceptive alternate routes to your hope.

In passionate, crazy faith, you speak or act in ways people may see as crazy. When others think your response is crazy, you ignore them because your eyes of faith have you captured or intoxicated with God's readiness to fulfill your heart's desire. In crazy faith, you unconsciously cut off all bridges that could lead you to alternate routes to the fulfillment of your urgent need. You only use the bridge to the Lord's mercy and supply. You cannot use crazy faith as a "camouflage vehicle" to prove you have strong faith.

LESSON: The *"camouflage vehicle" of crazy faith is to pretend to have faith, but behind the scenes, you use ungodly means to accomplish your needs.*

Camouflage faith is a deceptive, presumptuous pursuit of faith. It uses the name of Jesus as a cover over one's own fleshly striving for things one hopes. I am not talking about the convictions of faith that motivate your heart to pursue one action or another. God responds to crazy faith that pursues the course of actions in response to the Holy Spirit's leading in your urgent time of need. This course of action or path will always line up with God's will for you and it will not open you up to corruption. Jesus did not prove His faith when Satan enticed Him to turn a stone into bread or jump off the pinnacle of the temple (Matthew 4:2-7).

Again, I want to reiterate that faith is the assurance of things you hope to have. You do not see this hope but you convince yourself of God's ability and power to fulfill them in your behalf. This is what makes this kind of faith crazy! You see what you hope for with your spiritual eyes, your eyes of faith. It activates God's blessings and miracles in your life. Understand that God has already provided solutions to every need in your life. However, His Spirit nudges you to exercise your faith at the point of your need.

Your faith is the key that will open God's "storehouse" for your miracle or the fulfillment of your urgent need. God's "storehouse" is like a place in the Spirit where He keeps all the needs of men, especially His children. There, the angel of the Lord stands ready to deliver your need. Your faith is the key that opens the door to God's "storehouse".

The angel stands ready to deliver the need of whoever calls upon the name of the Lord. The size of the supply of your need is in proportion to the size of your conviction or the door your faith opens to God's "storehouse". Therefore, do not train yourself to doubt what the Holy Spirit quickens in your heart to ask from the Lord. If He asks you to ask for complete healing for your sickness, do not ask for anything less.

A father and son were driving home from an evening church meeting. Suddenly, the driver of a truck pulled beside them at a gas station and asked the father, money for gas for his truck. Immediately, the Holy Spirit quickened the father to tell the son to give him the gun he was holding. They did not have any gun but at that very moment, the Holy Spirit moved on the heart of the son to hand over a Bible he was holding.

The truck driver heard what the father said. He had gone to steal from someone's house and had no gas to drive his truck to where he was going. Therefore, when he heard the father say to the son, "Give me the gun", and saw the son hand over something to the father, he thought it was a true gun. Out of a guilty conscience, he ran away and left his truck behind. The father became very suspicious, and he called the police. The police came to pull the truck to their station.

When the father and son got home, he found his home burglarized! He drove quickly to the police station to report the burglary. One of the police officers suggested opening the truck to verify what was inside. When they did, everything inside the truck was from the house of the father and son. In crazy faith, the Holy Spirit sometimes gives you what to say or do in your critical times of need. Learn to do exactly what the Holy Spirit prompts you to do in your time of urgent need, even if it does not make sense.

Canaanite Woman with Crazy Faith

She was a woman from Canaan. Her example of crazy faith, recorded in Matthew 15:22-28). She came crying to Jesus saying, "Have mercy on me, O Lord, Son of David! My daughter is severely demon-oppressed" Jesus did not say a word to her. Nevertheless, this woman would not quit! She persisted in what she desired from Jesus.

The woman's persistence and unwillingness to quit got on the disciples' nerves. The disciples begged Jesus to send her away because she was crying out after them. Jesus answered them, "I was not sent except to the lost sheep of the house of Israel." The woman heard what Jesus said and she got personal with Jesus. She came and knelt before Jesus and said, "Lord, help me". Jesus answered, "It is not right to take the children's bread and throw it to the dogs". Wow, what a statement by Jesus; His statement did not deter the woman who was determined to get what she wanted from Jesus. She saw Jesus as the only solution for her need.

How many people in our today's church will endure when the man of God or the pastor refer to anyone as a dog? Will they not hit the door that very day and never return? In my ministry to the sick and the oppressed, there have been very few times someone has said to me, "I don't like the way you place your hands on my head." Wow! This is an indication of a person who is not crazy for God's miracle. They look for a nice way that anointed hands must be placed on them. If you have crazy faith for your urgent need, what do you care if the man of God anoints your eyes with mud he made from his saliva to heal your blind eyes (John 9:6)?

The Canaanite woman said to Jesus, "Truth, Lord: yet the dogs eat of the crumbs which fall from their masters' table." In other words, the woman was saying, "Yes, if I am a dog just give me what belong to the dogs— the crumbs from the master's table." At that statement, Jesus said to her, "O woman, great is your faith! Be it done for you as you desire." The woman's daughter received healing instantly. When you see a man or woman of God with a strong anointing, would you be bold enough to draw God's anointing from them to meet your need? In my evangelistic missions to the nations, I have seen in a few places where people with disabilities watch the power of God's presence come and go. They stay in their seats while others come and receive their healing. They never make a move to draw from the presence of God's anointing (which comes to bring their healing).

LESSON: *How crazy are you in your quest for God to meet your urgent need? Learn not to quit too quickly when the answer to your request delays or when God seems silent.*

The Canaanite woman persisted. She did not give up on her faith, notwithstanding the words of Jesus. This brings to memory another parable Jesus told about a woman who went to a judge to vindicate her. Initially, the judge would not help but she kept coming to him and would not quit. The judge realized he had to avenge her because her persistent bothering would wear him down (Luke 18:4-5). Though the judge was unjust, he yielded to the woman's persistence. Should not God avenge His own elect who cry to Him day and night, though He has been long-suffering over them? Jesus says God will avenge you speedily (Luke 18:6-7).

Then Jesus made a very powerful statement in the form of a question. He asked, "Nevertheless, when the Son of Man comes, will He really find faith on the earth?" — (Luke 18:8b). Jesus' question is ringing throughout the ages, from the past through today, and until He returns. Will Jesus find people with strong tenacious faith who will never quit despite the things that confront them in their faith journey?

When Jesus returns, will He find people who have tenacious faith? People who take God's promises by the "neck" and do not let go until they receive their heart's desires. God will surely come through for you if you persist in faith for your righteous needs. Jesus said God would help you speedily.

You have to learn crazy faith! Though your life situation may seem dismal, yet God wants you to speak life into it. You, woman of faith, why is it, in the eyes of the world's understanding, your biological clock seems to have run out and yet you speak faithfully of a husband you do not see? Why is it, man/woman of God that though the doctor has given you a negative diagnosis, yet you speak the opposite and continue to speak life into your body? It is because you serve the God whose Word of promise is true and will outlive the heaven and the earth.

Perhaps your need has nothing to do with your body or for a wife or a husband. Maybe it is for a job or for financial breakthrough. Realize that the enemy seeks to press hard against your hope to see if he can discourage you. He knows that if he can discourage you, your heart will begin to doubt and you mouth will speak negative words about your hope.

Those who get discouraged can distrust and quit on their God. Sometimes, you wake up in the morning and he tries to fill your thoughts with a sense of stalemate and defeat. Do not let him discourage and dampen your hope. In such times, learn to wake up with songs of praise to your God. Tell of His greatness in fulfilling your hope. This is the time you prophesy into your own life concerning your hope. Speak creative words about your needs and your expectations.

LESSON: *When you are intoxicated with your crazy faith in God's ability to perform a miracle for you, you declare things, which are not as though they are. People could call you crazy, but it is all right because they cannot see what you see. You see with your spiritual eyes of faith.*

Elisha's Crazy Faith

If you desire to walk with God, be ready to tear down your 'political correctness.' Oftentimes, what the Holy Spirit tells you to do for your breakthrough may not always conform to the norm. If you always expect what He does for you to line up with your emotional expectations, then you may miss your miracle from God. Oftentimes, God's instructions that lead to your breakthrough may not line up with your way of thinking. So learn how not to miss your opportunities for the miracles that you need, which will glorify God.

After his servant picked up the leprosy of Naaman, he met the sons of a prophet, who were willing to come under Elisha's charge. They asked Elisha's permission to go cut some lumber from the Jordan to enlarge the place where they live. Elisha gave permission to proceed and agreed to accompany them at their request. At the Jordan, the axe head of one the servants fell into the river and it sank to the bottom. When he showed where the axe fell, Elisha cut a stick from the tree and threw it on the water. Immediately, the axe head floated on the water (2 Kings 6:1-7).

This is beyond the comprehension of science. It is a well-known fact that if iron falls to the bottom of a bulk of water, like a river, you need someone who will dive in, go to the bottom to get the iron. You cannot cause iron to float on water! The iron head floated on water because the man of God placed a stick on the water! This is how God works sometimes.

LESSON: *Correctly orient your faith in God, the Creator of the Universe, and do not put Him in a box according to how you expect Him to work for you or manifest His glory on your behalf. With Him, all things are possible. He can make an axe head float on water!*

Your life situation may seem impossible, but do not see it as such. See it through the eyes of faith. Let your trust and hope dwell on the God with whom all things are possible! He caused the iron to float on water just because someone believed in Him to do exactly what the Holy Spirit instructed. If you have an impossible situation in your life, what is God saying to you? What is He telling you to do? Do not let the fear of failure and doubts kill your God-ordained miracles in your life.

Start declaring God's Word of promises that address your situation. Though things may not change immediately, be crazy enough to keep speaking into your situation. Then suddenly, you will understand the power of the identity you have in Jesus Christ. If the answer to your request delays, understand that your faith could be in a stretching mode. Orient your mind and heart to help you endure the stretching so you will not quit on God before your miracle. Be ready to endure to the last minute (if that is required).

Crazy Faith—Example of a Friend

A friend told me about what happened just before one of his mission trips. When the time for the mission came up, he did not have the finances to make the trip. Their ministry account was in the red. While his wife was trembling with anxiety, he assured her, "God will provide!" Truly, a day before the scheduled mission trip, he received a call from a friend to come out for lunch. During their time out, the friend not only gave money for his ministry, but also promised to take care of the cost of the mission trip!

If you wish to pursue God with a crazy faith, you have to learn to endure in your trust in Him to the last hour. Endurance is one of the attributes God has commanded to make every effort to add to your faith (2 Peter 1:6).

Strong Conviction—Strong Faith

Remember what your God says to you—decree a thing and He will hasten to fulfill it. However, you have to see what it is that you want with the eyes of faith. God asked the prophet Jeremiah, "What do you see?" Jeremiah said, "I see an almond branch." Then God said, "You have seen well, for I Am watching over My word to perform it". Declare what your pressing need is and have faith that your God is in the process of bringing it to pass for you. Your strong conviction of faith activates Miracles. Therefore, you have to activate your miracle by your genuine faith declarations.

Suppose you live across a river and a hungry lion is attempting to cross over to have you for its dinner. The only way it can get to where you are is by a dangling bridge held together by a rope left behind by some mountain hikers. If the lion falls into the swift current of the river below, it is doomed. You do not just stand there and shout in desperation. You have to cut the rope so the lion falls into the river. The sharper your knife, the quicker the rope will give way and the lion will fall into the river.

LESSON: *In your time of need, the sharper your faith, the quicker your problem will drown and bow to Jesus. "When the enemy shall come in like a flood, the Spirit of the Lord will lift up a standard against him"* (Isaiah 59:19).

Your faith will be sharp because you have a strong assurance of hope and you are convinced of God's ability to meet your need. You are convinced of His Word and you believe in His ability to help you.

Blind Bartimaeus' Crazy Faith

Jesus said to Bartimaeus, "Receive your sight! Your faith has saved you" (Luke 18:42). Jesus said this because he cried to Him with a crazy conviction of faith. He heard Jesus passing by and he shouted out, "Jesus, son of David! Have mercy on me." The people around him attempted to silence him but he shouted even the more. How crazy do you become in your faith when your pressing need require God's attention? Jesus asks us all, when He returns will He really find faith on the earth.

LESSON: *In crazy faith, your conviction makes God your only source of help. Lose control to God and He will delight to take over. You do not design in your heart how God aught to work things out for you. You learn to take the little steps the Holy Spirit impresses on your heart.*

A strong conviction of God's promise is to see what you hope for as a guarantee, though your natural eyes have not seen what your desire. Because you regard your hope as a guarantee, your inner being or spirit switches to a state of conviction for the things you hope. This is very important in both "living" and "situational" faith because you cannot hope for things you can see.

Obstacles to "Crazy" Faith

The Bible says in Hebrews 11:6, "Without faith it is impossible to please God. For this reason, you cannot allow your flesh, devils, and the world and people convince you crazy faith does not work in your day. They seek to diminish your passion to live by faith.

If you think it is politically inconvenient to take a crazy stand to move your faith forward for your urgent need, you might just give up your crazy faith. Usually, crazy faith produces miracles. Therefore, to walk before God and to please Him, you must be ready to participate in some faith fights. Faith fighting means you overcome doubts and worldly convictions that take your heart away from sound strong convictions of God's promises in His Word. Then you can walk in crazy faith. I will consider some obstacles you must learn to overcome in order to walk in crazy faith.

1.   Worldly Ideas and the Words of Man

Oftentimes, when the heart is not fully sold-out to God, it is possible the views and words of people can intimidate your pursuit of crazy faith. If the blind man in Luke Chapter 18 had yielded to the words of the people, he would have missed the greatest opportunity to receive his sight.

I will first consider a lesson from 1 Samuel Chapter 17. In this chapter, Jesse, the father of David, sent him to go give victuals to his brothers on the battlefield. Eliab was the elder brother of David and he was a soldier on the battlefield. When he saw David speaking to the men at the warfront, his anger kindled against David. He said to David, "Why have you come down? And with whom have you left those few sheep in the wilderness? I know your presumption and the evil of your heart, for you have come down to see the battle" (1 Samuel 17:28).

The words of Eliab did not assist David accomplish his God-ordained moment but to discourage him. If you let the words of man affect you emotionally, you are likely to withdraw from fulfilling God's purpose for your life's moment.

LESSON: *When God is about to lift you up to your new place of prominence, some people will despise you, and some will be angry with you without any justifiable cause. Some of them will wish that you remain in your low place and not step up onto the path that leads to your greatness.*

2.   Double Mindedness

Double mindedness is to have a mind that is not solid in your belief of God's ability to help you. Double mindedness always has an alternate route because he presumes God could fail. The Bible says if you ask anything from

God, do so with no doubt. If you are double-minded and unstable in your faith in God, you will not receive anything from Him (James 1:6-8).

To doubt is to be unconvinced of God's integrity to fulfill what His Word says or promises you. God is the only One in the whole universe whose integrity is beyond question. You cannot embark on a crazy faith with a mind that doubts God's integrity or His ability to fulfill His promises.

3. The "Voice of Rabshakeh"

Whenever you desire to embark on crazy faith, the spiritual enemies of your faith will whisper discouraging arguments in your mind. This is what I refer to as the voice of "Rabshakeh", 2 Kings 18:19-37. They will tell you all the reasons why you cannot be successful in your crazy faith. They will try to convince you that it is futile to trust God, and therefore suggest you to take their deal for your success. The following is an excerpt from the words of Rabshakeh in 2 Kings 18:22-25, "But if you say to me, 'We trust in the LORD our God,' is it not He whose high places and altars Hezekiah has removed, saying to Judah and to Jerusalem, 'You shall worship before this altar in Jerusalem?' Come now; make a wager with my master the king of Assyria: I will give you two thousand horses, if you are able on your part to set riders on them. How then can you repulse a single captain among the least of my master's servants, when you trust in Egypt for chariots and for horsemen? Moreover, is it without the LORD that I have come up against this place to destroy it? The LORD said to me, 'Go up against this land, and destroy it.'"

Does this sound similar to the tricks that the devil sometimes plays on your mind to convince you cannot trust God? In the wilderness, the devil took Jesus to a very high mountain and showed Him all the kingdoms of the world and their glory. Then he said to Jesus, "All these I will give you, if you will fall down and worship me" (Matthews 4:8-9). Note that this deceptive voice of the devil rings in the world today. Learn to identify his voice and do not become a victim.

4. Be Yourself

The encounter between David and his elder brother Eliab was significant (1 Samuel 17:29-30). David said to him, "What have I now done? Is there not a cause?" David turned away from Eliab toward another, and spoke in the same way, and the people answered him again as before. You hold the key to whether or not you will allow offense to derail your match towards your opportunity for greatness. Be focused and turn away from the object of offense.

LESSON: *When God is in the process of revealing your greatness, man's words cannot hinder you if you learn to "turn away" from the sources of hate and offense. Refuse to succumb to hurtful words and behavior against you.*

In life, you can be an "Eliab"—the one who takes offense at people God wants to lift up to their place of greatness—or you can be the one who assists them along the way. Recall the experience of Joseph during his captivity in ancient Egypt. He had the opportunity to interpret Pharaoh's dreams because the butler he met in prison told about his experience with Joseph.

Because David did not allow Eliab's discouraging words to affect him, someone eventually told King Saul about David's inquiries. David told King Saul how he killed the lion and the bear to rescue his father's sheep. God prepared David for his day of prominence away from people. At this moment, King Saul was convinced of David's claims after he heard his resume. The rest was history: David overcame the Philistine giant with the weapon that gave him his past victories and not with King Saul's armor.

LESSON: *Do not despise your days of private (behind the scenes) accomplishments, where no one was around to give you accolades. Also, do not try to imitate someone else's image when God is lifting you up to your place of greatness.*

Learn to be yourself and God will use who you are to accomplish His specific divine purpose. Instead of King Saul's armor, David took his staff, five smooth stones, and his sling—the instruments of his past victories! With these minimum tools, David was able to take down the giant.

LESSON: *God can use whomever you are and whatever you have, to do whatever He wants to do through you. Learn to be yourself.*

Shadrach, Meshach, and Abednego
(Daniel 3:15-25)

These three Hebrew men, Shadrach, Meshach, and Abednego, face the test of their faith in the God they had never seen. King Nebuchadnezzar said to them to fall down and worship the idol he had made. Nebuchadnezzar threatened them with a burning fiery furnace. With their faith in the God, they served, Shadrach, Meshach, and Abednego refused to bow to the king's idol.

The king commanded they heat the furnace seven times more than normal, to frighten the three men to give up faith in their God. The king said to the men, "If you do not worship, you shall immediately be cast into a burning fiery furnace. And who is the god who will deliver you out of my hands?" Because the three Hebrew men would not change their position, they cast them into the extremely hot burning fiery furnace.

• **Great Faith on Display**

I love the confession of the three Hebrew men in Daniel 3:16-18! They said to the king, "O Nebuchadnezzar, we have no need to answer you in this matter. If this be so, our God whom we serve is able to deliver us from the burning fiery furnace, and He will deliver us out of your hand, O king. But if not, be it known to you, O king, that we will not serve your gods or worship the golden image that you have set up."

Their statement of faith in God infuriated the king. He ordered some of the mighty men of his army to bind the three Hebrew men and to cast them into the burning fiery furnace. Because of their faith confession in face of the problem, the fire of the overheated furnace could not hurt them (Daniel 3:19-23). Meanwhile, the strong men from the army who threw the Hebrew men into the furnace lost their lives because of the outburst of the heat. The three Hebrew men fell bound into the fiery furnace but were unharmed.

When he looked, King Nebuchadnezzar saw four men unbound, walking in the midst of the fire, and they were not hurt; and the appearance of the fourth was like a son of the gods—an angel of God. However, when the three Hebrew men came out of the furnace, only the three men came out. Wow! God had just performed a miracle just because three young men dared to believe God with strong convictions. There was no smell of smoke or fire on them!

God said through the prophet Isaiah 43:2, "When you pass through the waters, I will be with you; and through the rivers, they shall not overwhelm you; when you walk through fire you shall not be burned, and the flame shall not consume you".

LESSON: *The ability to maintain your convictions and faith in God in your pressing times will invite His overwhelming presence. His presence will quench any raging fires from the devil.*

Chapter 14
Identity and Living Faith

"For everyone who has been born of God overcomes the world. And this is the victory that has overcome the world—our faith." 1 John 5:4

One of the most difficult things for man to do is to give up his will for another to control or define how he should live. This is so because God created man to rule on the Earth. One mistake someone could make is to receive a promotion to manage a department within a company and from then on, refuse to obey company policy. This employee could lose his job and be replaced by someone else.

Living faith is a call to live for Christ as your Lord. It requires strict obedience to His voice. His voice is His Word and the will of His Father. You become a sheep of His fold. He says His sheep hear His voice, He knows them, and they follow Him (John 10:27). You follow Jesus through a life of faith in your entire Christian life. As a lifestyle, you learn to daily define your life issues by God's Word. Ability to live this way pleases God because in faith, you sell your self-will for God's will.

This is the calling or lifestyle God expects every born-again believer to live. It is a profession for anyone who desires the fullness of Christ to grow in. In addition to growing your own faith, Jesus has given us apostles, prophets, evangelists, pastors, and teachers. He did this to equip you together with the church to come to the unity of the faith and of the knowledge of Him, even to mature manhood, to the measure of the stature of the fullness of Christ in you (Ephesians 4:11-13).

God says to you, "whatsoever ye do in word or deed, do all in the name of the Lord Jesus, giving thanks to God and the Father by Him" (Colossians 3:17). To do all things in Jesus' name and to give thanks to God the Father requires faith because without faith, it is impossible to please God.

In living faith, you learn daily to approach God with a heart full of assurance and you hold firm to your confession of faith. Then you will discover God's faithfulness (Hebrews 10:22-23). If your faith wavers, you may not experience God's faithfulness because without faith, it is impossible to please Him (Hebrews 11:6). Because you hold fast your confession of hope without wavering, you will have enough strength to encourage others.

LESSON: *When you receive salvation and willingly offer yourself for baptism, you make a covenant with the Lord, which you have to learn to keep daily through a life of faith.*

Living faith overcomes everything the world will throw at you. It overcomes all the attractions, distractions, and lusts in this world. All that is in the world, the lust of the flesh, and the lust of the eyes and the pride of life, are not from God but are from the world (1 John 2:16). Consequently, anyone who claims God as Father and is a friend with the world is walking in deception. God says to His people in 1 John 2:15, "Do not love the world or the things in the world. If anyone loves the world, the love of the Father is not in him."

In living faith, you pattern your daily lifestyle, your choices, and decisions to align with the commands, the admonitions, and the counsel from God's Word. The Bible says, "All scripture is given by inspiration of God, and is profitable for doctrine, for reproof, for correction, for instruction in righteousness: That the man of God may be perfect, thoroughly furnished unto all good works" (2 Timothy 3:16-17).

Your identity in Christ makes it the more necessary to live no other way but by faith in Him. Living faith is a moment-by-moment obedience to God's Word. You learn to trust and live by His promises (2 Peter 1:4). In fact, the foundation of your spiritual status in Christ is irrespective of your social status, educational prowess, or anything in this world but on the Word and grace of God alone. You are therefore required to live humbly in this life. Apostle Paul came to discover this when he said in 2 Corinthians 5:15, "And He died for all, that those who live might no longer live for themselves but for Him who for their sake died and was raised."

Although you do not see God, you know Him by an inner illumination that He is true and faithful, a God you can trust. Hence, you yield and pattern your life by His Word and promises.

Among the many gods the Athenians served in Apostle Paul's day, was one that they labeled as, "The Unknown God". The God you serve and worship is not a dead god or unknown! He is not a god made by man's hands. He is not a god far away. He is closer to you than the clothing against your skin. He is the God who made all things in Heaven and Earth. He is the God who seeks your cooperation, so He can take you higher and deeper into His

Son Jesus Christ. You do not see Him because He is Spirit, but you can trust Him by faith if you live and walk by His Spirit!

LESSON: *The things we see very often, and frequently, could soon become common in our eyes. Never let your Christian life become common in your eyes.*

God is supreme! He called the universe into being. He is the God who took Israel through the wilderness for forty years, where there was no grocery store or a textile factory to help replenish their food and clothing. God wants to show you His faithfulness. He wants you to seek Him so you might feel after Him and find Him, though He is not far away from you (Acts 17:27). When you find God and trust Him with an inner conviction on a continuum, you will know and experience His kindness in ways deeper than the average person experiences.

Do not be like many who lack the awareness of God's presence with them. Consequently, they yield themselves to lifestyles that do not please God. Apostle John said, "No one who abides in Him keeps on sinning; no one who keeps on sinning has either seen Him or known Him (1 John 3:6).

Today, many have found God by an inner illumination because they did not lose hope in their groping for Him. Jesus said those who seek would find! Understand that you do not "know" God the moment you receive Jesus Christ as Lord. To know Him requires daily pressing in through diligence, a life of prayer, and a consistent obedience to His Word! Then Jesus, the Wisdom of God, will reveal God to your inner person. Revelation of God in your inner self gives you ability to know His ways. Your inner hunger and passion for God fuels the living faith. It burns in you like a newly found lover. Your life of obedience to God's Word increasingly makes Him more real to you.

LESSON: *Living faith is a belief system based on the Word of God, which motivates your daily life and lifestyle.*

Fight to Live by Faith

The Bible says in 1 Timothy 6:12, "Fight the good fight of faith. Lay hold on eternal life, to which you are also called and have professed a good profession before many witnesses." God wants you to fight daily to move your calling forward. The Christian life is a race, which moves forward by a life of faith. God keeps you to your inheritance because you life by faith (1 Peter 1:3-5). You fight against doubt, carelessness, and the discouraging arguments of your spiritual enemies. You fight to keep yourself from the ways of the world.

God wants you, His child, to come to that place in your life where your deep and sincere love for God drives what you do and how you live. The faith life, driven by awareness and knowledge of God's Word and power will stand the test of time. Stand strong in your life of faith because everyday places a demand on you to live faithful to your Savior.

Because God expects the Church to come to the unity of faith, denominational beliefs that divide must give way to the pure unadulterated revelation of God's Word. The Church will cease to promote the enticing words of man's wisdom that form the basis of the differences in denominational beliefs and hence divisions. Fight your own faith fight to keep yourself pure from denominational doctrines that diminish the power of your identity in Christ.

Growing the Living Faith

Let your lifestyle of faith have a sound foundation to grow on and expand. The Bible commands you to make every effort to add seven qualities to your faith as recorded in 2 Peter 1:5-7. I refer to these as foundational lifestyles. They provide a solid foundation that helps your faith remain consistent. These qualities are the following:

- **Virtue:**-high caliber of character, free from immorality
- **Knowledge:**-to gain much information of your salvation, your Savior, and the demands these knowledge places on your daily life.
- **Self-control:**-ability to restrain the flesh and the drives of self.
- **Steadfastness**-an inner resolve to remain true to the calling and demand of your salvation regardless of what you go through in life. It is the ability or an inner strength that helps you bear a prolonged life pressure or the influence of the world, even pain or hardship without giving up faithfulness to your calling in Christ.
- **Godliness**-growth in your ability to practice the godly character of your identity in life issues.
- **Brotherly affection**-friendliness and care for others.
- **Love**-have a feeling of affection for, care for and devoted to one another. Sometimes you consider others equally or better than yourself.

These seven foundational qualities produce stability in your life and keep you from an ineffective and unfruitful Christian lifestyle. It keeps you from falling. To fall is to attend church and probably be involved in some form of ministry and yet God's Word is unable to influence your moral life. In that case, the Word is unable to place any constraint on your attitudes, lifestyle, behavior, and thought processes.

Jesus said in Luke 13:24, "Strive to enter in at the narrow gate. For I say to you, many will seek to enter in and shall not be able". To enter at the narrow gate, let the Word of God influence your attitudes, behavior, and deeds. You may ask why you have to strive to enter in when Jesus has finished and done all that is necessary to get you to Heaven. Well, understand that after your redemption, every promise you have from God is an opportunity that you will fight with faith to possess. If you refuse to fight to maintain your faith, you will continue to live in the ordinary, with no righteous or godly testimony in your life to tell of the faithfulness of Jesus.

The Bible refers to the experiences of the children of Israel from ancient Egypt to the Promised Land as a lesson or an example for the church of today. With many of the children of Israel, God was displeased and He overthrew them in the wilderness (1 Corinthians 10:4-6). They all enjoyed God's goodness in the wilderness but some of them did not make it to the Promised Land. Some of them were lustful, idolaters, and some tempted God. Instead of cooperating with God through faith, they lost sight of what He was doing for them and through them. They lost insight into the purpose of their deliverance. Consequently, God was not pleased with them.

LESSON: *To tempt God is to know His will and His promise of goodness towards you but inwardly or outwardly, belligerently despise or question His ability to do so for you.*

After your redemption, it is your responsibility to visit the throne of grace frequently to receive mercy and find grace to help you lay hold of God's promises through faith. Because you know your identity in Christ, be a part of those who choose the narrow-gate lifestyle irrespective of the hardness and difficulties that come with it. I believe you are one of those who have faith to help you endure the narrow gate lifestyle.

The narrow and hard way that leads to life is the way of godliness and righteousness, holiness and truth, all lived out through a life of faith in God's Word. These are difficult lifestyles to live on a continuum in this corrupt world. However, you are not one of those who presume on who they are and have in Christ, and fail to live the lifestyle that purifies them. Heed God's command to add the seven life qualities to help strengthen and stabilize your life of faith. Understand that your identity in Christ makes God's presence with you very powerful.

Never let God's presence with you become a vague notion, oblivious to its reality. You are in Christ. Therefore, choose to live an unwavering life of righteousness, which will create a spiritual platform on which your spiritual life and faith will grow stronger. On this spiritual platform, you will receive strength to withstand the temptation to stray away from the practice of godliness and holiness. With God's grace, defy the pressures this world may bring on you to deviate from growing a strong life of faith.

Living Faith—Examining Self

The Bible says in 1 Corinthians 11:31, "For if we would judge ourselves, we would not be judged". Again, in 2 Corinthians 13:5, God calls on you to examine and test yourself whether you are in the faith. You voluntarily place yourself under trial! Therefore, test yourself! You know yourself, including any hidden lifestyle, more than anyone else does. Know who truly drives your daily inner attitudes and motivations. Allow the Spirit of Christ to be the One who directs your inner attitudes and motivations because of your identity in Jesus Christ. You know yourselves, whether Jesus Christ is in you—unless indeed you have failed to acknowledge you are failing. God do not want you to live a life that disqualifies you from obtaining your inheritance in Christ.

After salvation, it is important to heed God's command to examine yourself constantly. Apostle Paul discovered how a Christian could be disqualified in the last day, if self is left unchecked (1 Corinthians 9:27). God wants you to examine your life for two things:

- Whether you are in the faith
- Whether Christ is in you

To test whether you in the faith, you test for a genuine pursuit of the Gospel of Jesus Christ. Test if the Gospel is what defines or influences your daily life issues in your choices, decisions, and deeds. Your faith is genuine if your trust in God remains solid and untainted both in your good times and in the various kinds of trials that may come your way.

LESSON: *One of the difficulties of man is holding on to hope he does not see.*

God does not intend any of your life difficulties to destroy you. Rather, His goal is to grow your faith in God so you can endure to the end to receive your hope of righteousness—reward for righteous lifestyle. You do not see this hope now. That is why you have to pursue it with a daily life of faith. When your faith withstands the test of time, it produces in you a glorious character in the eyes of the King of Heaven. It makes you appear as gold polished and tested by the fires of life. Your appearance will be glorious and honorable when Jesus returns (1 Peter 1:6-7).

In living faith, the Gospel of your salvation or God's Word becomes the driving influence in your daily choices, decisions, and lifestyle. Let it influence your thought processes and views of life and of people because as a man thinks, so is he (Proverbs 23:7). Since you do not see the God you serve, pursue Him with conviction in His Word. Convince yourself that He exists and He rewards those who seek Him diligently. Know He is with you in every moment of your life issues and is ready to help you. In His greener pastures, He supplies your needs (Psalm 23:2).

Testing for the Character of Christ

The passage in 2 Corinthians 13:5 commands you to test if Christ is in you. Christ desires to find a comfortable home in your life. Christ is the power you need to confront and overcome the storms of life. The evidence of His presence is a life of obedience to Him and your humble approach to life and His kingdom. Jesus said, "Take My yoke on you and learn of Me, for I Am meek and lowly in heart, and you shall find rest to your souls" (Mathew 11:29).

A yoke is equipment hung on the necks of bulls. As these bulls move in specific directions, they turn the soil, making it ready to sow seeds. The yoke of Jesus is His meekness and lowliness. He says these qualities will orient you for a life of rest in your soul.

Therefore, when you test yourself, look for meekness and lowliness. When you yoke two bulls together, the stronger bull will do most of the work. If you take Jesus' yoke on you, His overwhelming power acts on your behalf. It takes you beyond where your natural ability ends. You have nothing to worry about when you share Jesus' yoke, except to walk in faith and trust. It is a win-win life for you, irrespective of all that the world will throw at you. Therefore, do not buy the world's idea that meekness and lowliness is a sign of weakness. Rather, see it as a sign of spiritual maturity and strength.

LESSON: *The help you need to know Christ is not necessarily the abundance of knowledge of His Word but more so the influence His Word has on your life. It makes you a woman or a man of faith.*

Your submission to God's Word through a life of obedience provides you with divine wisdom to know God by revelation. It also enlightens your spiritual eyes. The presence of Christ in you comes with some benefits. I will consider a few here:

1.   The Spirit of Wisdom and Revelation of God

For all who seek after God, it is His will that you find and know Him as Jesus did. Jesus said in John 8:55, "You have not known Him. I know Him. If I were to say that I do not know Him, I would be a liar like you, but I do know Him and I keep His Word."

The statement, "I know Him and I keep His Word" is significant. Earlier, I said that to keep God's Word is to obey His Word. Obedience to God's Word is proof that you know Him and believe in Him. First John 2:4-5 says, "Whoever says "I know Him" but does not keep His commandments is a liar, and the truth is not in him, but whoever keeps His word, in him truly the love of God is perfected. By this, we may know that we are in Him."

Jesus said He would reveal Himself to the one who keeps His commands. In addition, Jesus is the wisdom and power you need to know God by revelation. Therefore, if you keep His commands (His Word), He, Jesus Christ, the wisdom of God, will lead you into the knowledge of God.

To know God by revelation, pray for a good heart in addition to your knowledge of His Word. This is so because under the new covenant, God wants to write His law in your heart (Jeremiah 31:31-33). The book of Proverbs calls on people to treasure God's commandments; to incline their ears to the wisdom it provides, and to apply their hearts to understanding. If they cry out for knowledge, lift up their voice for understanding, and seek it as they would for silver and search for it as they would for hidden treasure, they would understand how to walk in the fear of the Lord and find the knowledge of God (Proverbs 2:1-5).

LESSON: *Avoid the temptation of becoming proficient in matters of Church but fail to grow in your ability to obey God's word.*

2.   Enlightenment of Spiritual Eyes

Having enlightened eyes is a dimension of sight that you receive in your heart from the Lord. It enables you to see things beyond the natural sight; you see with your inner spiritual eyes—the eyes of your heart. It activates spiritual understanding of life occurrences. It strengthens your hope and trust in God's Word and promises, though you do not see Him with your natural eyes. God is Spirit and those who worship Him do so in spirit and in truth.

First Corinthians 2:14 says, "But the natural man does not receive the things of the Spirit of God, for they are foolishness to him; neither can he know them, because they are spiritually discerned". God is Spirit and people who dwell on fleshly motivations will always miss Him. In fact, people motivated by the flesh cannot please God.

Enlightened eyesight gives a spiritual touch to the eyes so it can filter the things that come through the eye gate. This way, it will feed the mind with only information that fortifies your heart for a stronger life of faith rather than corruption of the heart. It will help the heart to discern and accept what God does by His Spirit. The natural eyes do not see what the Spirit of God is doing. It causes the heart to doubt God.

The enlightened eyes will feed the mind with the righteous and edifying things of life. The mind will then help the heart develop strong convictions of the hope set before you in your Christian calling. It helps you or gives you the ability to differentiate between the wealth of your heavenly inheritance and the competing inheritance from the world, which is passing away. Your ability to make this differentiation helps the mind understand how important your calling in Christ is and catch the revelation of the immeasurable power of Heaven that backs your daily life.

3.   The Enlightened Eyes and Interpersonal Relationships

Because your enlightened eyes can see, you know and have confidence that the immeasurable power of God has you covered in life situations. You can say with King David that the Lord is on your side and you will not fear. What can man do to you? The Lord is with you and He is your helper. You will look in triumph on any enemy that comes against you (Psalm 118:6-9). Your enemies are not people but devils who use people to intrude into your space, seeking to interfere with God's purpose for your life. These enemies use people to cause you to trip up, in an attempt to destabilize your righteous stand in Jesus.

You have to learn from Jesus! He told the disciples how the elders, the chief priests, and the scribes were going to reject and kill Him. Apostle Peter rebuked Him for saying such things. However, He did not rebuke Peter but Satan. He knew Judas was going to betray Him, yet He fellowshipped with him and was not harsh on him.

Your enlightened eyes can "see the thousands of angels encamped around you", and you will not entertain the idea that someone is out to get you or hate you. Your emotions and attitudes in your interpersonal relationships will flare up if you have the idea that someone hates you or is out to harm you. Take refuge in the Lord and trust in Him and do not trust in the security of self or self-aggrandizements. The security of self can give you a "touchy" attitude in your interpersonal relationships.

A man or woman with enlightened eyes receives a revelation of where people live and therefore is able to handle offense correctly in the fear of the Lord. The Bible says the friendship of the Lord is for those who fear Him (Psalm 25:14). People's attitudes and behaviors do not negatively influence your emotions. The things people say and do to you, or fail to do for you, do not affect your stability in Christ Jesus. He is your refuge and your fortress.

It is the fear of the Lord that helps you relate to people in a way that is righteous. It helps you in this world to serve God acceptably. Therefore, the fear of the Lord is a requirement for all people irrespective of religious affiliation. It is by God alone all people live, move, and have being, for all people are His offspring, irrespective of nationality, gender, or race. The Bible says in Psalm 33:8, "Let all the earth fear the LORD; let all the inhabitants of the world stand in awe of Him!"

LESSON: *The fear of the Lord is to have a little or a large amount of the knowledge of God and His requirement for your life. Then allow this knowledge to influence how you live, in order to please Him.*

If you have the knowledge of God and His requirement for your life, and you fail to honor Him with what you do in life or by your lifestyle, it is an indication that you lack the fear of the Lord.

When the eyes are enlightened spiritually, you gain the ability to view life issues from both the natural and the spiritual points of view. It helps you make godly decisions and choices in life. The things you see in this world are transient, but the things you do not see are eternal. Therefore, handle correctly the things you see to God's pleasure.

Living Faith and God's Greener Pastures

In His life, Jesus knew Satan had nothing good to offer Him in His pursuit of the Father's will. This is a mindset you need for your life of faith. If you think the world owes you something, you will be tempted to yield to her corrupting lifestyle.

LESSON: *Your conviction and knowledge that Satan has nothing good to help you fulfill God's purpose in life is the first step to your victory over corruption in this world.*

God has an inheritance for you in Christ. He has provided you with all you need from His "greener pastures", His pleasant place. In God's pleasant place, you receive His covering and abundant supply just as the sheep receives the most nutritious feed in the greener pastures. If you pay careful attention to your life in Christ, you may come into some seasons where you could feel elated and supplied with the good things you desire, notwithstanding the difficulties and persecutions.

Do not be like certain people who, unfortunately, switch to attitudes and lifestyles that cause them to stray away from God's pleasant place in life. Consequently, they get into wilderness experiences very often. This is God's way of getting them back to faithfulness.

Find God's pleasant place for your life because there, He restores your soul regardless of any painful thing the world may throw at you. In God's pleasant place, your life gains stability in your faith. He leads you in the path of righteousness for His name's sake. You will fear no evil in seasons when your life walks through the valley of the shadow of death. You will fear no evil, for God's presence will always protect and avenge you. Therefore, learn to stay in God's greener pastures irrespective of what goes on around you or in your life.

God is jealous for His name and power that He has invested in you. Even though you walk through the valley of the shadow of death, He even prepares a table before you in the presence of your enemies. He will anoint your head with oil for protection and for strength (Psalm 23:3-5). In your calmness of faith in God, your enlightened eyes become sharp for your daily Christian walk.

Living Faith and the Promised Inheritance

By virtue of Christ's resurrection, God has given you a new birth. The new birth comes with the hope of an inheritance that is alive. This inheritance is imperishable, undefiled, and unfading. God has kept this inheritance in Heaven for you. God has elected (by His foreknowledge) that you will receive His call and live with a sanctified spirit that will motivate you to walk in obedience to His Son Jesus Christ (1 Peter 1:2-4). Now, consider the following:

• Test of Genuineness of Faith

The inheritance set before you is unfading and incorruptible. It is a sure promise! Therefore, learn to endure in your life of faith so God's power will keep you safe until you attain to the inheritance that He has ordained for you. It does not imply that you will not encounter challenges and trials because you walk in faith. The many trials and challenges you go through will not destroy you but will test the genuineness of your faith. Faith is not just the words you proclaim but also a life you live. This is how God's power keeps and guards you to your inheritance (1 Peter 1:3-7).

You know that life's challenges and trials test your faith. For this reason, you need to learn endurance so you can do God's will to the end to receive what He has promised (Hebrews 10:36-38). In a very little while Jesus will return and will not delay. As God's righteous child, you need to pursue genuine faith because those who draw back from faith will fail to satisfy God's pleasure. It is God's will that you attain salvation and the glory of Christ when He returns.

• Keep Hope Alive

Understand that hope is something you do not see in the now. Your hope is for Christ's return and attaining to His glory. To keep this hope alive, you have an obligation to live a pure life. First John 3:2-3 says, "Beloved, we are God's children now, and what we will be has not yet appeared; but we know that when He appears we shall be like Him, because we shall see him as he is. And everyone who thus hopes in Him purifies himself as he is pure." Failure to keep hope alive could cause many to default to life as usual, and fail to pursue purity of self.

To keep the hope alive, you cannot fail to purify your life—soul, spirit, and body. You learn to live by faith, where you define your life issues by God's Word. The great Savior you hope for is pure and He says, "Be holy for I Am holy". Your hope for the return of Jesus Christ is not the same thing as depositing a large sum of money in the bank and leaving it to earn interest while you do nothing.

God's command is to cleanse yourself from all defilements of body and spirit and to mature in holiness through the fear of God (2 Corinthians 7:1). In your daily life, you have to have the ability to prove what is excellent, so you can remain pure and blameless until the day of Jesus Christ (Philippians 1:10). Therefore, purity of life through a daily walk of faith will keep your hope alive. Learn to get your heart far from evil declarations. Everything about God in Christ towards you has the aroma of love for people. He declares wellness over your life because you have an identity in His son. Learn of Him and do so to other people.

Chapter 15
Identity and the Normal Christian Life

Believe Me that I Am in the Father and the Father in Me, or else believe Me for the sake of the works themselves. Truly, truly, I say to you, whoever believes in Me will also do the works that I do; and greater works than these will he do, because I Am going to the Father.—John 14:11-12

Jesus referred to and acknowledged God as the source of all He did in His life on the earth. It was the power of the presence of His Father with Him—"the Father in Me." He said to the Jews, "My doctrine is not mine, but His that sent Me" (John 7:16).

Jesus wants believers to abide in Him and Him in them because we have an identity in Him. Your identity in Christ makes you God's special individual, and God expects you to have an accurate knowledge and belief in the doctrine of Jesus Christ. Incorrect knowledge and belief will stifle your ability to walk in the power of your identity in Christ Jesus. On the other hand, accurate belief in Christ's doctrine can influence your life for the better. It opens you up for the manifestation of the power of the Kingdom to which you now belong.

Therefore, refuse imprisoning yourself in traditions that have nothing to do with the Kingdom of God. God wants you to begin manifesting the greatness He has destined for your life in this world and the world to come. Because you have a new identity in Christ, refuse to clothe yourself with a cold mundane religion that fails or doubts what Christ has ordained you to be and to do. God wants you and His Church to help people come to the saving knowledge of Jesus' Gospel. God wants you and the Church to heal the sick, cleanse lepers, raise the dead, cast out demons, open blind eyes, and to heal the cripple and the lame.

LESSON: *Your greatness in this world does not come from an abundance of financial or material wealth that you may have, or even an abundance of scriptural knowledge. Your greatness begins when the nature of Christ in you begins to enlarge. Therefore, refuse to live as though this world is your heaven.*

The journey to the fullness of your greatness depends on your cooperation with God. You acknowledge Jesus as Lord and you walk in Him, rooted and built up in Him and established in the faith (Colossians 2:6-8). God helps you along this journey.

God's Family of Power Brokers

You have to grow in the attributes that make you a part of God's family of "power brokers". That is what you have become through your identity in Christ Jesus. Jesus said you would receive power when the Holy Spirit comes upon you (Act 1:8a). God's desire is that you will live and grow in your belief in His Son. God has a promise for you! If you live by His Word and promises you will become a partaker of His divine nature and hence, a part of the divine "power brokers". You will be able to do what Jesus did while He was here in our body. You function in this world but also in heavenly realms.

God expects you to participate in His system of power, not only in the age to come but also in the world today! He gives this to you as a foretaste of who you are going to become when Christ returns—a ruler. If you acknowledge and understand who you are now and who you are going to become, you will not live or entertain a mentality as Esau did. Esau mentally diminished the importance of his destiny and his inheritance. Jesus said, "Behold, I give to you authority to tread on serpents and scorpions, and over all the power of the enemy, and nothing shall by any means hurt you" (Luke 10:19).

The prophets of old were great men of God. Nevertheless, Jesus said that though John the Baptist was the greatest among all those born of women, he who is least in the Kingdom of God is greater than he (Luke 7:28). Praise God! You are in God's process to conform you into the image of the greatest—Jesus Christ. Your status in God's Kingdom will make you greater than the greatest prophet the world has ever known. This is a very exciting revelation! However, it places a demand on you to cooperate with God in His conformation process to make you into greatness.

Elijah was the prophet who called down fire to consume his altar in his contest with the prophets of Baal. When the Lord took him away with chariots and horses of fire, he left a double portion of his anointing for Elisha. Joshua came after Moses and did greater works. King Saul killed his thousands, but David his ten thousands.

Jesus was greater than any known prophets, even Moses was. Moses was faithful in all God's house as a servant, but Christ was faithful as a Son. You are part of His house, if you hold fast the confidence and the rejoicing of the hope that you have in Him, firm to the end (Hebrews 3:5-6). Before Jesus left to go to His Father, He said you also could do the works He did and even do greater works if you believe.

Can you see the spiritual trend here? The work of God goes from a lesser to a higher and greater glory. God said through the prophet that the glory of His house would be greater than the former (Haggai 2:9). Jesus commands believers to go into the entire world and proclaim the Gospel to the whole creation. He says whoever believes and is baptized shall receive salvation, and many signs will follow him (Mark 16:17-18).

Seeking Answers

According to John 14:12, Jesus said that those who believe in Him would do the works that He did and more because He was going to the Father. To believe is to entrust your mental, physical, material, financial, and spiritual well-being to Him. It is to commit everything in your life to Him: your health, your future, and all your expectations. In believing, you come into a new state of being because in Him you live and move and have your being (Acts 17:28). You become the offspring of Abraham, the father of faith.

LESSON: *If Christians are the people, who believe in Jesus and who receive the baptism of the Holy Spirit, then what Jesus is describing is the "normal Christian life".*

Meanwhile, why is not every Christian doing as Jesus did? What could possibly be the reason that not all Christians are manifesting the power of their new identity, as stated in Mark 16:17-18? The Bible says the Kingdom of God is not just talk but power (1 Corinthians 4:20). The power that accompanies the Gospel you have received places a demand on you to submit to a life of truth, righteousness, godliness, holiness, and mental purity.

The Kingdom of God is not just intellectual proficiency and verbal capabilities in the Word. Sometimes much knowledge puffs up the ego (1Corinthians 8:1). Apostle Paul's speech and preaching were not with enticing words of man's wisdom, but in demonstration of the Spirit and of power of the Gospel (1Corinthians 2:4).

Has the preaching of the Gospel shifted in emphasis? Has the emphasis shifted to the proclamation and not in demonstration of its power? Through Apostle Paul, the Spirit said the time was going to come when people would have a form of religion but would deny its power.

Apostle Paul was the man who walked in truth and the power of God and used righteousness as a weapon for the right hand and for the left (2Corinthians 6:7). The demonstration of the power of the Gospel demands some discipline in truth, love, and a level of holiness.

Learn not to substitute the demonstration of the power of the Gospel with your intellectual proficiencies. Jesus demonstrated both and He expects you to do likewise. Therefore, the state of your inner personality along with your knowledge of the Gospel and the Gospel you preach aught to harmonize. Do not be the Christian who becomes very proficient in the knowledge of the Gospel, yet has serious issues with the expressions of the inner personality.

There is contention between the Word preached and the ability to practice the Word known. This is where the power of the Gospel comes in to set people free from hidden inner spiritual issues. In 2 Corinthians Chapter 7, the Lord calls on His people to cleanse both their body and spirit from all that defiles.

Because you have an identity in Christ, God expects you to grow up spiritually, mentally, and in your godly lifestyle. This way, you will not only become proficient in proclaiming the word of the Gospel, but you shall also manifest the power of the Gospel. Walking in the power of the Gospel brings completeness to the Kingdom proclaimed.

Jesus sent the disciples and said to them, "And as you go, preach, saying, 'The Kingdom of Heaven is at hand.' Heal the sick, cleanse the lepers, and raise the dead, cast out demons. Freely you have received, freely give" (Matthew 10:7-8). Whenever the preaching of the Gospel of the Kingdom goes forth, demonstration follows, which confirms what Jesus says in verse 8.

Getting the Belief System Right

Jesus says you and I have the capacity to do what He commands in Matthew 10:7-8. Therefore, if you fail to do so, then the problem lies with you and not His request. Learn to check your belief system. Check the foundation you have built in your heart for God's Word. Check if the problem is not because you have an incorrect approach to the Kingdom. Check if the problem is incorrect personal and interpersonal relationships, attitudes, or pride and arrogance. Is it divisions and differences in doctrinal beliefs that are out of line with God's expectation? Is it denominational competitiveness, which is stifling the Kingdom's power?

LESSON: *The power of God's Kingdom is very vast in comparison with the power Christ wants you to manifest in your life. God wants to gain glory in the* *world through you, though you are insignificant compared with His Kingdom. Therefore, do not let your denominational doctrine or yourself grow too big in your eyes. Otherwise, you will not fit your "God-ordained doorway" that leads to the greater anointing God has for your life.*

Through a heart of humility, learn to live tough and endure hardness as a good soldier of Christ. Consider these points. See if they can help you.

- Do not lack understanding of the demands the kingdom life and your identity in Christ place on you.
- Do not train yourself to gravitate towards convenience in your Christian experiences.
- Do not allow the "horns" of the devils deny you anything the Lord has ordained for your spiritual life.
- Ensure your attitudes, behaviors, and lifestyles in your personal and interpersonal relationships are not causing you to deviate from God's expectation for you as a born-again Christian.
- With humility of heart, address issues in your Christian life that deviate from godly and righteous standards of God.
- Do not only know of God's word but also believe and practice.

The prophet Nehemiah, the scribes, and the Levites taught the children of Israel the law of God. When they understood what the law said, they began to weep. The prophet Nehemiah told them to cease mourning because the day was holy unto the Lord. He made them understand that the joy of the Lord was their strength (Nehemiah 8:8-10).

Under the New Covenant, everyday is a holy day. Do not therefore lose your joy at anytime. The Bible says to rejoice always, which require a correct and godly view of all that happens in your life. This is one of the ways to maintain your praise and your peace in the Lord, irrespective of what goes on in your life. It is Kingdom-mindedness!

The Bible commands you to strive for peace with everyone. Your peace and joy will activate praise in your heart for your Savior, Jesus Christ, and for your salvation. Do not lose your praise, your strength, or your peace! These life dispositions, both in the spiritual and in the physical, are very important for walking in your greatness.

The prophet Zachariah saw a vision recorded in Chapter 1, verses 18 to 21 "Then I lifted up my eyes and looked, and behold, four horns! And I said to the angel who talked with me, What are these? And he answered me, These are the horns that have scattered Judah, Israel, and Jerusalem. And Jehovah showed me four craftsmen. And I said, What are these coming to do? And He spoke, saying, These are the horns which have scattered Judah, so that no man lifted up his head. But these have come to terrify them, to throw down the horns of the nations who lifted up their horn over the land of Judah to scatter it."

The enemy of your greatness comes against your Judah, your Israel, and your Jerusalem! Your Judah is your praise and worship, your willingness to rejoice always. Your Israel is your strength and your determination to prevail as a prince with the power of your identity in Christ. Your Jerusalem is your peace of mind and body. God wants you to live by the power of His Spirit so you will grow your ability to speak to your mountains to move!

The enemies of your greatness must not continue using their "horns" to hinder the power of your identity in Christ Jesus. You must daily declare who you are in Christ Jesus! Let the whole world know you are the child of the God of all gods. Tell yourself, "I am a member of God's "power brokers" in the earth!" Tell yourself, "I am the child of God!" Tell yourself and see yourself as a king and a priest of God (Revelation 1:6). See yourself as part of a special species of creation. You are a chosen race, a royal priesthood, a part of a holy nation, God's own possession.

God wants His qualities to flow out of your life as it did through His Son Christ Jesus. God wants you to cast down the lying arguments of the devils (2 Corinthians 10:5-6). He wants you to owe no one anything except love. He wants you to have nothing against anyone. He wants you to lay hands on the sick and see them recover. He wants you to fear no foe except the temptation to limit yourself in who you are in Christ. View limitations as enemies!

God wants you to defy your enemies by rejoicing in the face of problems. Never buckle in the face of any problem in your life because your God sets a table before you in the presence of the enemies of your identity. God says to you in Philippians 4:4, "Rejoice in the Lord always; again I will say, rejoice." He wants you to cast out demons! He wants you to speak in a new spiritual language! In the name of Jesus I say to you, "Begin to speak in your new spiritual language right now!"

Build Confidence in God

God's craftsmen come to terrify and to throw down the horns that come against your "Judah", your "Israel", and your "Jerusalem". Identify the things that limit your ability to function (just as Jesus said you should). Identify where your trust in God is lacking. Get back to those things that excited you in Jesus Christ when you first accepted the Gospel.

Refuse to allow the horns of the enemies of your greatness get you back to the things you gave up when you first understood the Gospel. Do not allow them to silence your praise and worship with sickness or diseases. Do not let them stifle your strength and your peace. Keep your daily life under the covering of the Lord through your life of obedience to His Word.

You need all the strength you can get from Jesus to believe His Word. Your obedience will help you step into and function in the realm of His Kingdom power, which is what He expects of you. The loss of a job, marriage, or difficulties in your life or ministry must not stifle your praise, your worship, and your peace. Ensure your limitations are not because of a lifestyle of pride, an attitude of irritation, or corruptible ways, which could be hiding in your life and away from others. You have determined to walk in your identity in Christ. Therefore, God's craftsmen will always overwhelm the enemies who lift up their horns against His purpose for your life.

LESSON: *Life problems or difficulties must not cause you to switch to uncertainty or unfaithfulness. Your problems are no match for God's power to bring you solutions. God sent four craftsmen against the four horns that came against Judah, Israel, and Jerusalem. God will overwhelm the horns that interfere with His purpose for your life.*

Suggested Prayer

Dear Father in Heaven, I stand in the name of Jesus Christ and I lift my hands to your throne of grace. I ask for forgiveness in the areas of my life that I have ignored. Now, I declare I understand my identity in Christ. I know who I am in Christ Jesus and I ask for grace to walk in the power of my identity in Him. I apply the blood of Jesus to any stronghold the enemy has legally gained. I declare that the blood of Jesus and the fire of the Holy Spirit tear down and off all the horns of the enemy against me. Thank you for answering my prayer.

Author Contact: WorthyLamb Ministries International
Web: http://www.worthylambtech.com
Email: worthylambministry@sbcglobal.net

Other books by author

Awaken to your new creation
ISBN: 978-60034083-3

Living Above
ISBN: 978-1-58169-338-6

Re-Created for Greatness
ISBN: 978-1-4497-2421-4